KEEPERS *of the*
TESTIMONY

KEEPERS *of the* TESTIMONY

FAY ROWE

KEEPERS OF THE TESTIMONY
By Fay Rowe

ISBN-10: 1-897373-14-7
ISBN-13: 978-1-897373-14-9

All scriptures, unless otherwise noted, are from The Authorized King James Version, The World Publishing Company, Cleveland and New York, 1945. Used by permission.

Cover Image: Gillian Fritzsche
Cover Design: Nikki Braun & Gillian Fritzsche
Interior design: Larissa Bartos

Published by Word Alive Press
131 Cordite Road, Winnipeg, Manitoba, Canada R3W 1S1

WORD ALIVE PRESS

Dedicated to my mother,
Mary Louise Sparkes.

*Like the honorable woman whom Proverbs commends,
her children arise up and call her blessed.*
~Proverbs 31:28

CONTENTS

ACKNOWLEDGMENTS

In the context of my foray into the world of writing and publishing, I've discovered a very important and comforting principle: We're not meant to do anything alone. God, who himself lives and works in relationship as the Trinity, Three in One, always sends mentors, helpers, critics, and encouragers to help get the job done.

You know who you are—you wonderful proofs of God's blessing and faithfulness—but I shall name some of you anyway.

Thanks, first of all, to the wonderful staff of Word Alive Press. Caroline Schmidt, in particular, made the process of getting this book out into the world a relatively painless experience.

Thanks to Pastor Jay Jayaraman for his kind words of endorsement. By word and example, Pastors Jay and Sarah Jayaraman inspire me to dream. They are true keepers of the testimony.

Thanks also to the members of London's Ready Writers' Group, headed up by our courageous leader, Mary Haskett. These friends—and especially, among them, my critique partner, Linda Greenberg—often kept my feet to the path when I began to grow weary. Their companionship on the road of writing is a priceless treasure.

My friends Ida Hall and Judi Smeltzer rose to the challenge once again in this new venture as they did so kindly in *What's in a Name.* Along with their encouragement and invaluable insights, Ida helped me choose a better word more than once and yet again saved me—or, at least, tried to—

from my love of commas, while Judi helped me find a place to hitch my horse when I was done. So also, my friends Sharon McMillan and Beth Burdick gave gentle critiques that made a difference.

There are others, dear family and friends, who always take their place in my cheering section no matter what my challenge or endeavor. I appreciate you all.

And finally, thanks to my husband and best friend, Glenn, and my daughter and son-in-law who brighten my days, Gillian and Ryan Fritzsche. All three have been of help in innumerable ways, from sharing encouraging words and much-needed counsel to creating cover designs and website pages. In all of these, they show their faith in my dream and motivate me to "go it again."

Every one of you is a gift.

I am blessed!

INTRODUCTION

"He made his own people to go forth like sheep, and guided them in the wilderness like a flock. And he led them on safely, so that they feared not...and he brought them to the border of his sanctuary...yet they...kept not his testimonies..."

~Psalm 78:52-56

The thought of sharing my testimony evoked terror in me through many of my early years. I mistakenly thought an impressive testimony—one, therefore, worth sharing—had to involve a dramatic change from a life of crime or at least debauchery. Consequently, having pretty much grown up as a Miss Goody Two Shoes in a home where God and church were high on the list of our most important influences, I figured I had nothing to say.

I remember feeling extreme frustration with my shortage of inclination and lack of ability to share my faith—a frustration no doubt exacerbated by guilt. As a teenager, I probably headed to the altar fairly often to repent of my falling short in this area. Of course, I always eventually got over the guilt—at least until another sermon on evangelism rekindled the shame.

However, years later, as my husband and I drove home from Grace Maternity Hospital with our little daughter tucked as securely as possible in my arms, I looked into our baby's eyes and knew with certainty that sharing my faith was about to become more than a performance by which my effectiveness as a Christian would be judged. Vastly more.

What I experienced that day is, almost certainly, common to all Christian parents. When we bring a new life into the world, instinct tells us that doing our part to help that young soul enter the kingdom of God must become a major priority in our lives. Within moments of our first sight of that little face, we make an inner commitment to someday share with that precious one the faith that guides our own life.

Early in the parenting experience—probably from our toddler's first emphatic "No!"—we face a frightening fact: Our babies have a will of their own. All too soon we realize that our children's decision to follow Jesus isn't a given and we can't legislate it. It remains their choice and, therefore, their responsibility.

However, the good news is that we can make their decision an informed one. Thankfully, there are biblical precedents which show us how to teach our children well and share with them the reason for our faith.

Experience and observation have shown me that we sometimes try to bring our children into the kingdom by dwelling on the laws of God. Perhaps we hope they will see how they fall short of God's requirements—in other words: their sinful state—and recognize their need of a Savior. However, while this book will not suggest we ignore training in righteousness, especially since God is our example in giving the law as a tutor, it will show that a large part of sharing our faith with our children is found elsewhere. It is found in our keeping of the testimony.

Testimonies are simply stories we tell about how walking with God has made a difference in our lives. That's all they are—stories. We all have them.

Many of our stories deal with small, seemingly insignificant events. We may think the events and, therefore, the stories have no importance to anyone but us, but that is not true. The testimonies that are ours to give—the accounts of God's involvement in our lives—have immeasurable value. That may be why there has been a spiritual onslaught against them from the very beginning.

It's true; our stories are enormously important. This book will show just how important they are to God, to our children, and to all who hear them. Hopefully, it will also challenge, encourage, and empower us to tell them.

To parents who might feel as if they have not been keepers of the testimony, I must say this: I know that by now you may want to put this book down, but please don't do it. Read it to the end. We parents are all alike in both our desire to be perfect and our inability to be so. This book has been written by one who, like most of us, has not always faithfully kept the testimony. We take comfort in the fact that what matters most in this, as in every part of our lives as Christians, is God's faithfulness.

Having said that, I must also add that I believe this book will give us an effective tool to use and, along with it, hope. As we read, let's not allow any sense of guilt to keep us from either. For most of us, our children's last chapter has yet to be written. Even if we feel we have already run out of time and opportunity, we must remember that none of us are privy to the inner workings of someone else's heart, even those of our own children. For that reason, we can still hold fast to our hope by remembering God's love for, and commitment to, the seed of the righteous (Proverbs 11:21).

As we go forward from this point we would do well to remember that the true influence of our testimonies may never be accurately measured on this earth. By God's grace we will see some of it, but our stories will probably affect the lives of some we will never meet and some who may never even hear the words we speak. Just as a stone thrown into a still pond causes ripples that repeat many times before they stop, so does the testimony have its effect, often in ways we will never see. Maybe in Heaven we'll see how far the ripples have reached.

We begin with a story. I hope you have a plentiful supply of grace to give me as you read.

CHAPTER ONE

~

Tell Them About Me

"I will sing of the mercies of the Lord forever:
with my mouth will I make known
thy faithfulness to all generations."

~Psalm 89:1

~1~

"I'M NOT PRAYING for them anymore. I don't care if they go to Hell!"

Those disturbing words begin the story of an event that changed my thinking and later became the seed of this book. They shocked my husband as I said them, but no more than they did me.

The words tumbled out of my mouth early on a dull, misty morning—not unusual for January deep in the heart of Texas—as I drove my husband to the university where he was in the second year of his doctoral program. I was one of two fourth grade teachers at a Christian school near the university and I was referring to two of my students. Glenn and I usually prayed for the boys as we drove to work in the mornings—probably more for my sake than theirs—but today I didn't want to. I had given up.

I loved teaching, and I especially loved teaching fourth graders. Still a kid somewhere deep inside, I had always enjoyed a good rapport with children of that age. They were more often than not enthusiastic, creative, open-hearted, and generally pleasant. I found it great fun, for the most part, to spend my days with them.

But for some reason—and I've never been able to pinpoint a good one—these boys were too much for me to handle. The sad truth was they got on every nerve I had. "Ten-year-olds from Hell," I called them on my worst days. I felt as if they were the source of all my troubles.

They were definitely the source of my sadness for all the parents who were paying good money to have their little ones educated in a Christian environment, only to have them influenced daily by my two nemeses; the source of my embarrassment that I was failing to keep control of my class; and—probably why my husband prayed so earnestly for the little darlings!—the source of the bad humor I took home every day.

The tension in my classroom grew daily. I was sure everyone could sense the hostility the boys felt for me. Even worse, I was afraid that the festering resentment I felt toward them might also be obvious to everyone—resentment I had tried unsuccessfully, time and time again, to overcome.

The parents of my other students were talking about my troubles. Some of them even sent me encouraging notes, telling me they were praying for me. That should have helped, as I'm sure it was meant to, but it just made me feel worse. I felt as if everyone knew those two ten-year-olds had effectively deposed me. Oh, how I wanted them gone!

Glenn went ahead and prayed while—yes, I'm embarrassed to admit it—I sulked.

In minutes, we were at the university and I sat alone in the car.

Ah, but not quite alone. There was God.

Suddenly and painfully aware that he'd heard what I said, I back-peddled.

"Lord, I'm really thankful for my job," I offered piously, and then couldn't resist this whine, "… but do you realize what a great year I'd be having if I didn't have those two terrors in my class?"

Not really expecting a response, I clearly heard this gentle thought, *"Where would you have me send them?"*

The hairs on my arms stood straight up even as my heart sank. *God* had sent them to me?

Now I was ashamed—ashamed I'd complained, ashamed I had been unable to help them, and probably most ashamed because I still didn't want them.

A scene flashed into my mind from the workshop I had attended just a couple of months previously, the theme of which was how to deal with strong willed children. Not surprisingly, the large conference room at the Loews Anatole Hotel in Dallas had been packed out, standing room only, with teachers desperate for ideas. It was a great seminar, filled with laughter and knowing nods as the speaker accurately and humorously described our children and our daily struggles with them. In the end, the speaker said simply, "If you don't love these children, you can't help them."

Pained silence! *Love them?*

One teacher, no doubt the most desperate of us all, had the nerve to raise his hand and ask, "Isn't there another way?"

I could hear my heart beat as the speaker considered her words. She sighed noticeably.

"No," she replied. "I know they aren't the most lovable kids in your class, but if you don't love them," she repeated the bad news, "you can't help them."

Now, several months later, unexpected emotion constricted my throat as I told God my shameful truth, "I don't love them. How can I help them?"

Then came this thought: *"To a ten year old, time is love. Give them your time."*

Pictures immediately came to my mind of scenes God must have sorrowfully watched unfold over the previous months. I saw myself in my classroom, talking happily with the other children whenever they came to me with their stories, but putting off these two boys because I didn't like their stories—their reports of Beavis and Butthead or whatever other, in my opinion, nasty TV show they loved—saying, "Tell me about that at recess time." As if any ten-year-old boy wants to chat with his teacher during recess!

The scene changed to our classroom morning devotions. I saw how I had tried to use the Bible as a behavior modification tool, encouraging the children to behave in a manner appropriate for young Christians—a manner which, as a very pleasant side effect, would make my life easier. When my tactic didn't work on my two hooligans, I tried to persuade the others not to follow their example. That didn't work either. Not for some of them at least.

Again, there was that quiet voice inside. It said simply, *"Tell them about me."*

I had known for months something had to change. Now the light of truth dawned: It had to be me! I was the one who needed to change! The revelation stunned me.

That morning I started. Somewhat reluctantly, I confess, I dispensed with my precious schedule and listened to stories—the good, the bad, and the ugly stories. Afterward, I read the Biblical account of David's confrontation with Goliath, and talked about what David must have known about God that made him take on someone who was probably several times his size.

Then we started math class.

The next day we repeated the process: First, their stories; then, God's story. Our mornings followed that format for the rest of the year. Every day brought a new story about God. When I ran out of God stories from the Bible, I told my own. When I ran out of my own, I told my friends' stories.

A few weeks after the change, at the end of devotions one morning, one of my Texan Terrors appeared to be day-dreaming instead of getting out his math book. I walked over and stood near him, just as a reminder of what he ought to be doing at that point. Jamie (not his real name) looked up into my face and whispered conspiratorially, "Miss, God is cool, isn't he?"

Amazed, I remembered a boy whose heroes only a couple of months earlier had been of somewhat questionable character. I smiled and nodded, silently thanking God this boy was beginning to find a new hero. This could only be good news.

Before long, I had the opportunity to put into practice the "time is love" advice, this time in a more challenging way than just not getting down to business as quickly as I'd like each morning.

It happened one day as my class settled down after recess. Two of my adorable girls started to tell me about their basketball team. Animated and enthusiastic, they caught me up in their excitement.

"I'd love to watch you play some time!" I exclaimed, not at all prepared for what happened next.

Jamie astonished me. He had heard my exchange with the girls and now, as cute as he was troublesome, he challenged with an impish grin, "I play basketball. Would you come watch me play?"

Time is love. Give them your time. Ouch! I could almost see the words in front of me.

I recognized an open door. Instinct told me to walk through it, but I didn't want to. I didn't relish the prospect of going out after dinner on a weeknight to spend even more time with this, my biggest trial in the form of a slight ten-year-old Texan.

"Sure I will. Just tell me when." I forced the smile as I said it.

"This Wednesday at 7 p.m.," he returned. The quizzical look on his face and the doubtful tone of his voice said he didn't quite believe I'd show up. Something that felt uncomfortably like guilt squeezed my heart.

That Wednesday, and pretty much every Wednesday of the season, I watched basketball at 7 p.m. At first I went out of sheer obedience and nothing more—except, perhaps, desperation—but before long I loved it.

Soon, basketball season ended and softball began. Every week I found a perch on the stands in the Texas heat and watched softball. There I sat and sweated and cheered, officially a fan but not necessarily of the game.

Then came one marvelous day when, during morning devotions, I talked to the kids about how God has good plans for each of them. I said, "I look at you and I see that so and so is great at mathematics, this one writes beautifully, or that one plays a fabulous basketball game. But I also see congressmen and congresswomen, businessmen and businesswomen, doctors, teachers, pastors, evangelists, and more."

Later that morning, Jamie brought me his math assignment to be checked. As I looked at his work, he stood quietly by my desk. Then, reaching out his hand, he touched my arm, leaned toward me, and whispered, "Miss, I'm the evangelist, aren't I?"

Trying to be nonchalant, I whispered back with more joy than I let him see, "I wouldn't be at all surprised!"

After our closing assembly on the last day of school, the children came back to the classroom to receive their report cards. That done, we chatted about summer plans for awhile and they teased me about having to read their names from my prompt sheet during part of the assembly. Finally, the dismissal bell rang. Amidst hugs from the girls and general mayhem as my almost-eleven-year-old boys felt that first rush of freedom, we said our goodbyes. I felt that mix of emotions every teacher has at the end of the final semester—glad the school year was over, but sad at the same time.

I stood outside for a while watching my students pile into their parents' waiting cars. Then, enjoying the anticipation of my own version of freedom, probably better described as peace and quiet, I strolled back toward my classroom. When I reached the gravel patch where our outdoor lunch tables sat, I paused to chat with one more mom. We were still visiting when, out of the corner of my eye, I saw Jamie run back up the concrete walk. I sighed, thinking he'd lost his report card and now I'd have to go hunting.

He politely waited until the parent had left. Then he ran over to where I stood and leaned on my side.

A Texas side-hug! Jamie wanted a hug.

As we stood there on the gravel, my arms around his shoulders, I managed to get out, "I love you, Jamie. You know that, don't you?"

I meant it.

First, a pause; then came the quiet response, "Yes Ma'am. I love you too."

What God hath wrought! My eyes brimmed and my heart was full.

As he scooted back down the walk toward his waiting mother and sibling, he threw back over his shoulder, "There's a game Friday. You comin'?"

"Sure will! See you there!"

I think we both knew it would be the last time. He was no longer one of my kids.

My other Texan Terror's story, complete with open-hearted moments, sorrowful tears dripping from two chins, and gifts of hopefully-not-stolen Canadian tea, is just as close to my heart but better left for another day.

Ever since then, I've been convinced that God's two directives, "Give them your time," and "Tell them about me," were what made the difference in the lives of two wannabe wayward ten-year-olds and their cranky teacher, whom God's grace had brought together so all three would learn something.

I hope the boys learned that God is a good God who loves them. That was, eventually, what I wanted them to learn. I also hope that before all was said and done that year they felt that love from me.

My own lesson was unexpected and priceless. I learned that when God said, "Tell them about me," it was because those boys needed to know him—to know his character—just as much as, or maybe even more than, they needed to know his laws.

Ever since that year with my beloved Texan Terrors, I've been convinced that the wisdom of God's instruction to me was not particular to my circumstance or to those children. The truth is we all need to know him, and his plan has always been that those who do will "Tell them about me" and do it in love.

Each of us has a part to play in the destiny of those who come into our life, as they do in ours, and a very important aspect of our role is the story—the testimony—we share.

There can be no doubt we will need God's help to play our part well, but we all can be keepers of the testimony.

THINKING ABOUT CHAPTER ONE

SELF DISCOVERY QUESTIONS:

1. Do you see yourself as part of the destiny of the men, women, and children in your life?

2. Do you think of them as having a role in your destiny?

3. Have you thought much about the role you/they have been called to play?

KEEPERS' PRAYER:

Dear Lord,

Open my eyes. Help me see the people in my life as you do. Help me to be humble enough to learn from a child.

CHAPTER TWO

~

Tell Me the Old, Old Story

"Thy testimonies are wonderful:
therefore doth my soul keep them."

~Psalm 119:129

~2~

MY MOTHER IS THE CHIEF keeper of the testimony in our family.

Those who know our family might assume it was my father. Dad was a cash crop farmer who loved his Bible. He read and enjoyed all kinds of books but he loved his Bible best and read it voraciously. Well known in our parts for teaching the precepts he found there—or attempting to, at least—to anyone who'd listen, Dad took every opportunity that presented itself to spend time with friends, believers or non-believers, talking about whatever great truth he was studying of late.

I can still see him standing near the fence which surrounded a field of young cabbages or carrots, talking Bible with a neighbor—quite possibly Uncle Hayward Bradbury, Dad's best friend, who wasn't really our uncle but who got the title since he was (as were all the men in the church) Dad's brother in the Lord, or perhaps a member of one of the other denominations in town, or one of the unchurched neighbors—who'd stopped by to ask how the crops were coming along. Dad enjoyed sharing his secrets for growing what we considered to be the best crops in the area but I sometimes wonder, since the Bible was his passion, if the fellow-farmers or back-yard hobbyists had to listen to his sermons before they got his secrets.

Nevertheless, while my father was all about ideas and doctrine, my mother has always told the stories. That may be because story-telling is largely a feminine trait, relational in its motivation. This un-researched but nevertheless quite plausible hypothesis is of my own making and unscientifically supported by the fact that some of my favorite childhood memories are of the times my mother's sisters visited.

Mom and her three sisters rarely had the opportunity to get together since two of the four siblings had years ago moved to the mainland of Canada. On those few occasions when the long overdue and impatiently-awaited visits happened, and after one of my mother's legendary turkey dinners, a description of which could never live up to the exquisite reality, my older sisters and I would linger at the kitchen table while our mother and her sisters told stories—the aunts all the while diligently picking every last morsel from the leftover carcass of the ill-fated bird. They would talk and laugh for quite some time—at least as long as the pickings of the bird of the day lasted, which was still never long enough for me—reminiscing about their youth and childhood.

The girls and their four brothers had grown up during the Depression years. Their father had left their small village in order to find work in the United States, so they were raised by a practically single mother. Poppa did his best to send money and clothes but life still challenged the family. In spite of the hardships my mother and her sisters endured, probably daily, their stories made it sound as if growing up almost penniless in an isolated Newfoundland village offered the most exciting life possible for a child.

I loved listening to them reminisce, and not just because their tales—some of them, perhaps, quite tall—gave us fascinating insights about our mother and left us howling with delight. It was also, in part, because their stories about family history gave me a sense of belonging.

I'm convinced that family stories give children the feeling of being part of something bigger than themselves and, somehow, that translates into a sense of value. The sense of belonging created by stories like those of my mother and her sisters was important even back then in the closely knit cultural fabric of our small town, and is probably even more so in the fast paced, everything-mobile lifestyles of today.

However, as crucial as are the tales about Grandmother's antics and Great Aunt [*insert name of your own most eccentric great aunt*]'s high jinks, more important still—and, I dare repeat, especially so today—are the stories which recount the family's walk with God. These stories give a child the sense of being part of something far greater than the family. They give a real sense of identity as one who was planned and beloved, and not just by parents.

Perhaps that last comment explains why my favorites of all of my mother's stories were those that told what God had done in her life.

One fall night, sometime in the early 1930's, thirteen-year-old Mary Louise Antle knelt at a chair during a young peoples' meeting at her pastor's home in the village of Victoria and gave her life to the Lord. Then and there, my mother promised Jesus she would "never go back on him" and, by God's grace, she never did. That was the first of her stories and many were to follow—like this next one.

I don't recall which year it happened, but it was when my brother Byron was still a very small boy. My mother and I had taken a train trip on the old Newfie Bullet to Badger, a town in the center of the island, to visit our former pastors. I felt pretty special being the only one of five children allowed to go on this trip, although years later it occurred to me that it may have been because I was an irritant to my three older sisters and had to be taken out of their way. Nevertheless, the trip was very exciting and on Friday, as arranged, my father joined us for the weekend.

In the wee hours of Sunday morning we received a call from the sitter at home saying that Byron had developed blood poisoning from a cut on his head. My parents hurriedly packed up and we left immediately. It would be a long drive home over almost 250 unpaved miles, interrupted by a brief time put up at a pastor's house in a town some distance down the road while we waited for the dawn ferry ride across the Exploits River.

Through the long hours of the night, I slept in my mother's arms. I awoke occasionally and when I did I'd hear my parents praying out loud. My mother would sometimes whisper softly, "Pray for your little brother." I had never been asked to pray before so I knew it must be serious. That and the obvious fear in my mother's voice scared me.

When we got home late that afternoon, we found Byron miraculously recovered from a dangerously high fever and other frightening symptoms and playing contentedly on the floor with the same cans of Carnation milk that had crashed on his head a few days earlier. Since 20/20 hindsight is a wonderful teacher, this time he played with just a few. This time the tower wouldn't get so high. I'm pretty sure it was the following Christmas that he got his Mechano building set.

I'm not sure if I remember that story so clearly because I was there or because I heard it so often. My mother repeated it fairly regularly in the years following the incident. No doubt it came to her mind frequently since the scar on Byron's head, an interesting quarter moon shaped indentation, was quite noticeable because of the very short brush cut Mr. Cave, of Cave's Barber Shop, gave him every Saturday. (It may not have been quite that often but my memory banks hold altogether too many tortured vignettes of sitting in Mr. Cave's shop waiting for Byron's turn to have his head shaved.)

As time went on and children and then grandchildren grew, life as matriarch of a large family provided my mother with plenty of other stories to tell. Several of her favorites relate to employment. It has always seemed to me that my mother's prayers for her children's and grandchildren's employment received special attention in Heaven, perhaps because of her importunity. She refused to give up. She had no doubt God wanted them gainfully employed—common sense told her that, as did the apostle Paul's directive that he who doesn't work, shouldn't eat (2 Thessalonians 3:11)—so she was never concerned about being too forward with the Almighty.

Once, after one of her grandsons had moved to another province in order to look for work, she requested prayer for him from a guest speaker at a conference she and my father were attending. The speaker picked up her prayer request out of the many in his hand and mentioned it: "Here's a grandmother asking God to provide a job for her grandson."

That encouraged my mother, telling her God had heard her prayer. From that moment, she didn't worry.

The following week when my sister told her how anxious she was about her son, Mom mentioned the prayer request and said, "Don't worry about a thing. He'll have a job by Friday. Mind, now,"—this meant you shouldn't argue with her—"you can mark my words. He'll have a job by Friday."

To this day my mother doesn't know why she said that but, sure enough, on Friday the call came. My nephew had a job which, at the time of this writing, has long since turned into a very lucrative career.

On another occasion, one of her grandsons had applied to join the police force. He had been waiting for quite some time to hear if he had been accepted, and by now serious discouragement had set in. My mother prayed earnestly for him, even staying home from the too-public church prayer meeting so she could have the time and privacy to do so.

While visiting my sister's home one evening, she asked my nephew, "Did you get that call yet?"

"No," he replied despondently, and went on to tell about others who had already been informed of their acceptance.

"Don't you worry about a thing! You'll hear soon," she asserted with something very like prophetic fervor.

My father, not wanting him to get his hopes up only to have them dashed, tried to help out by telling him he was just as good a man outside the force as he would be in. Even though my mother was *very* disturbed by this apparent lack of faith in her prayers, she kept quiet about it and "held her tongue," confident that time would vindicate her.

Sure enough, a couple of days later my nephew received a call from the police headquarters asking when he could come for his uniform fitting and training schedule. Surprised, he told them he wasn't aware he'd been accepted. Apparently, someone had forgotten to make the official acceptance call.

Ah, vindication is sweet, and answered prayers even sweeter.

My mother even tells a few stories about my father. One of my favorites is about the time he procrastinated in giving attention to an ailing septic tank. Apparently she nagged him about it for quite some time, and then, finally, said to the Lord, "I'm not asking him anymore, Lord. You know I need that taken care of, so now I'm asking you. You're going to have to take care of it." I'm pretty sure she wouldn't say, "Mind, now!" to God, but I imagine he knew she was thinking it.

Half an hour later my father came in and picked up the phone.

"Who are you calling?" she queried. (I'm not sure of this scene, but I can imagine her glancing up from a floured board covered with plump raisins buns, expecting a request that she drop everything and deliver eggs to a customer.)

With a determined look on his face he answered, "I've got to get someone to look at that septic tank!"

My mother smiles broadly when she tells that story.

Whether she tells her stories deliberately with a desired result in mind, or whether she tells them because they bring her joy, my mother continually passes on the accounts of our history and, with many of them, the witness of God's faithfulness in her life and in the life of our family. She doesn't leave any question as to who brought the blessings into her life, saying, "No glory be to me. All I did was pray."

I love my mother's stories. They tell me much more than her words relate. Interwoven in the fabric of her tales, I see a vivid picture of someone who knows God loves her. Raised without the presence of her earthly father, she somehow became keenly aware of the love and care of her Heavenly Father and developed an unyielding expectation of his faithfulness. This expectation remained, in spite of the times her prayers didn't result in a desperately desired end.

In listening to my mother's testimonies, I eventually recognized the source of her confidence. I saw the security she felt as one who belonged in the family of God. Through the sacrifice of Jesus, God had invited her in and long ago in her pastor's living room she had accepted her place in the family. Instinctively, she knew her Father God didn't love anyone more than her.

I'm pretty sure that just as my father wanted to share the truths he loved, so my mother has always wanted to share with her children and grandchildren something that has blessed her own life, and so, throughout the years, she has told her stories.

What a gift those stories have been to me! In their telling, my mother taught me that I can have that same confidence in God's care because I, too, am precious in his sight.

As much as I enjoy my mother's stories, I believe God enjoys them even more.

Actually, I know he does. God is all about stories.

THINKING ABOUT CHAPTER TWO

SELF DISCOVERY QUESTIONS:

1. Do you have a heritage of faith in your family?

2. If not, are you ready to start one?

3. Can you think of stories you have been told or can tell?

KEEPERS' PRAYER:

Father,

Thank you for the testimonies I have heard throughout my life. Help me to share my own stories of your faithfulness.

CHAPTER THREE

~

"I know Abraham."

"Give thanks unto the Lord: call upon His name;
make known His deeds among the people.
... Remember the marvelous works that he has done;
his wonders and the judgments of his mouth."

~Psalm 105:1, 5

~3~

IT'S TRUE. STORY TELLERS have always been big with God. In fact, once upon a time, long, long ago ...

No, I mustn't start that way, because even though we sometimes look at Bible stories—especially those in the Old Testament—almost as if they were myths or fairy tales, it really was on a *particular* day and at a *specific* place that God chose a storyteller to be his partner in the covenant that would begin the process of bringing the world's Redeemer to earth.

That man was Abraham, and this is the beginning of the story he told.

It began in Ur of the Chaldeans where he was born. Abraham—whose name was Abram back then—grew up there as did many of his forefathers, and it was there, sometime after his marriage to the beautiful Sarah, that Abraham heard from God.

Historians tell us that the people who lived in and around Ur were moon worshipers. Although the Biblical account of Abraham's call and subsequent journey doesn't mention that particular and rather peculiar aspect of his religious life, I can imagine that the occasion of the Lord God speaking to him must have come as quite a shock to Abraham.

Can you picture it? I doubt that it was in a huge ziggurat temple of worthless worship that Abraham heard God. I prefer to imagine the event happening outside in the cathedral God built, where the heavens declare his glory. Maybe the animals were especially restful that night, and the air cool, still, and quiet. Perhaps the sky was clear and bright, filled with stars and flooded with moonlight. It may even have been while Abraham considered the impotent moon that he heard instructions from the one true God to leave his family behind and go on to the land of Canaan, "to a land that I will show you" (Genesis 12:1).

We don't know how God spoke, whether in the still small voice we're familiar with or in an audible voice most of us have never heard, but we know Abraham heard him.

Think of it! Not in church and not by the mouth of a prophet, God spoke to a moon worshiper. Actually, we read in Acts 7:3 that the Lord God *appeared* to Abraham. We probably can't quite imagine that but, nevertheless, whatever the manner or means of the communication it must have made quite an impression because Abraham, the moon-worshiping heathen, obeyed.

Well, sort of.

Told to leave his family behind, Abraham nevertheless took his father, Terah, and his nephew, Lot, with him on the journey—maybe hedging his bets since he wasn't yet intimately acquainted with the God who had spoken. But to his credit, hedging his bets or not, off he went.

They didn't make it all the way, possibly because Terah was too old or unwell to travel. Instead, they eventually stopped in a place called Haran where they all lived until Terah died. After the death of his father, Abraham continued the journey to Canaan.

Surely, God must have been aware of this potentially problematic character flaw—the tendency to partially obey. Yet, in spite of it, he chose Abraham to be the one with whom he would make the covenant that would legitimize Jesus' entry into the earth. Years later, Abraham's act of faith and obedience in being ready and willing to sacrifice Isaac would give God, as Abraham's covenant partner, the legal open door to offer his own son as sacrifice for the sins of the world.

How ironic that this paragon of near-obedience, Abraham, was the one who would eventually become known as the father of our faith!

I have often wondered, "Why Abraham?" I know there could be discussion at this point about an all-seeing omniscient God who is outside of time, but most of us who aren't quantum physicists just can't quite grasp that concept. Besides, the stories of the Bible are given to time-and-space-bound mortals who are surely supposed to take away from them some understanding of God's ways that will make sense back at the house after Wednesday night Bible study is over.

So, again, why Abraham?

An event which occurs later in the story and is recorded in Genesis 18:17-19 clearly tells us one reason God chose Abraham:

"And the Lord said, Shall I hide from Abraham that thing which I do, seeing that Abraham shall surely become a great and mighty nation, and all the nations of the earth shall be blessed by him? *For I know him that he will command his children and his household after him, and they shall keep the way of the Lord*, to do justice and judgment; that the Lord may bring upon Abraham all that which he hath spoken to him."

"For I know him," said God. The word *know* in that passage has been translated in some versions of the Bible as *chosen*. In other words, the translators are saying God *chose* Abraham in order that he would command his children.

While this is no doubt true, the word for *know* used there is translated everywhere else as meaning *possessing knowledge*. I'm convinced God was saying he *had knowledge* that Abraham would set up a precept for his household—as the word translated *command* also indicates—that said they would keep God's ways. It would become the defining characteristic of their family identity: "Our family follows God's ways."

Abraham would command his children and, as we see in retrospect, teach and train them to walk with God, and God chose him expressly because he would do so.

God had a plan and, it seems, in order for it to be successful he needed someone he could trust to pass on the knowledge of both his presence and his plan to the generations to come, because such knowledge would be crucial to the lives and destinies of those generations.

Even though our modern concept of commanding is probably fraught with negative connotations, any good parent will recognize that commanding is part of the early training of our own children.

However—and I imagine most modern parents will agree with this as well—commanding alone wouldn't be enough. Commanding would not be sufficient to ensure that the desired behavior would continue after Abraham left the scene. God needed a teacher, which connotes much more than being a commander, and he had found one in Abraham. No doubt, the fact that Abraham would take the time to teach his children to keep the way of the Lord appeared as a huge plus on his resume.

God also needed a story teller because, as we have subsequently seen in biblical records, much of the training and teaching Abraham needed to do involved story telling. God surely must have been confident that Abraham would tell his children the stories of his walk with God, beginning with the account of the first time they met. Evidently, since we still hear the stories millennia later, God's confidence in Abraham was not misplaced.

God knew that in commanding, teaching, story-telling, and, no doubt, modeling, Abraham would inspire his children to walk with God themselves. A huge part of the emerging plan was that as Abraham's children walked with their father's God, he would become their God too, and they, in their turn, would walk in his blessing throughout their generations. A crucial factor in the success of God's strategy would be their strong desire to walk with God; therefore, such a desire had to become securely embedded in their hearts.

God was confident that because Abraham would train and teach his children, those children would learn to follow after their father's God. Because of it, God would not only be able to bless Abraham but he would also eventually bless the earth through him. The ultimate outcome: The blessing of mankind with salvation through faith in Jesus. (We shouldn't be surprised, should we, that God is the ultimate long-term goal setter?)

From the moment he met the Lord God, Abraham's blessing began. We know from our own reading of the Bible that to be blessed is to be empowered in some way; as time went on it became obvious that a huge part of Abraham's blessing was found in empowering knowledge.

Although Abraham had probably grown up worshiping the moon, he had now met the creator of that moon and, as a result, was about to be blessed with knowledge others didn't yet share. Before long, Abraham would know the moon wasn't his source *of* life or his source *in* life and it didn't deserve his worship. God would soon show Abraham that he, God, possessor of Heaven and Earth, was that source.

A vastly important piece of information!

Knowledge effectively acted upon is powerful, and as we look back on Abraham's life we can see the amazing empowerment he experienced when he found out that the real strength of his life was his friendship with the Lord God.

As if that wasn't enough, God blessed Abraham with a calling, a purpose in life. Despite the fact that it would take some time for Abraham to become the man of faith and obedience he could be, God chose this less than fully obedient moon worshiper to participate in the most important project he'd initiated on the earth in some time. God actually chose a moon worshiper to help him set in motion the whole plan for mankind's redemption.

It boggles the mind.

Chosen, because he would keep the testimony!

THINKING ABOUT CHAPTER THREE

SELF DISCOVERY QUESTIONS:

1. What might history say about your walk with God?

2. Have you ever felt you needed to be perfect in order to be useful to God?

KEEPERS' PRAYER:

Lord,
I'm thankful I don't have to be perfect to walk with you. Thank you that you look at my willing heart and not at my history.

CHAPTER FOUR

~

The Testimony Service

*"Blessed are they that keep His testimonies,
and that seek Him with the whole heart."*

~Psalm 119:2

~4~

I GREW UP LISTENING TO TESTIMONIES. It happened, with regularity that rivaled the sunrise and sunset, every Sunday morning and evening in the little peaked-roofed church at the head of the pond in Shearstown, the town where I spent my childhood and youth, and which sits almost as quietly today as it did then in a green valley between two hills on the predominantly rocky east coast of Newfoundland.

Every week I sat on a wooden pew—usually with my friend Lois, and probably on the half-pew by the stove where we hoped we wouldn't be noticed, hidden as we were by the black pot-belly—and, along with fifty or so grownups and children, I listened to testimonies.

The testimony service has pretty much fallen out of favor in recent years, but if they were part of your childhood you probably remember them distinctly. However, just in case someone reading this book has not experienced one, we'll go back there for a minute or two.

The church service itself would begin with two or three preliminary soul-stirring hymns, the last of which most likely included words such as "I love to tell the story of Jesus and his love," after which the song leader would signal the start of the testimony service with a question: "Who has a word on your heart for the Lord?"

If no one immediately volunteered, as was sometimes if not often the case, the song leader would put an end to the awkward silence by starting up a chorus—as opposed to a hymn which had three, four, or five verses as well as a chorus sung, sometimes repeatedly, after each verse.

Usually, after that, a few members of the congregation would stand one at a time, decently and in order, to tell about their conversion experience or some recent blessing they had received from God, spiritual or otherwise. On a particularly good day several might stand at once and have to wait their turn. Of course, the testimonies were interspersed by more choruses.

The testimonies were usually short and simple but, I feel compelled to admit, not always either one. Still, they were usually both.

Sometimes the testifiers would merely repeat the verse of a hymn or a chorus which expressed their heart better than they could themselves. Afterward, the song leader might lead us in a rousing rendition of the same chorus. A favorite, I recall, included these words:

"I remember the time. I can show you the place
Where the Lord came in and saved me by his grace.
I cannot tell you how, but I can tell you now,
Jesus saved me. I know he saved me."

The presentation may have been simple, but I recall what an indelible impression was made on me when I heard elderly men and women—elderly, that is, relative to me since I was a child—talk about God's faithfulness.

It didn't matter if they were educated or uneducated, cerebral or emotional, sophisticated or unrefined. They always impressed me with the fact that after a lifetime they were still willing to—no, happy to—give witness to God's goodness. Their testimonies created a vivid picture in my mind of how Christianity was supposed to work, and that it simply ought to be that "whosoever will" (Revelation 22:17) can have a life blessed by God's presence, no matter what he or she encounters on the journey.

Sometimes, we heard the same people testify and the same testimonies shared every week. That may have been because they felt they owed it to God to speak for him and not let the opportunity of a testimony service go by without expressing their gratitude for all he had done. That, of course, would be an excellent motivation by any standard, and since good news of any kind bears repeating, a repeated testimony wasn't a serious issue.

But, to be fair to the faithful, I will say I suspect that sometimes—depending on what the leader thought his duties consisted of—these good people stood to testify in great part because they were cajoled to do so. Or it may have been that they expected the service and choruses to drag on for at least an hour, as they did in some instances, and they knew it would be an excruciating experience for all of us if no one got up.

That may be why the testimony service fell out of favor, and probably why many of us might consider that fall a good thing. I confess I am torn. Sometimes I miss them. They were, more often than not, inspiring. When they weren't, they were at least entertaining!

Today's testimony services are far different. Almost never spontaneous, they are, instead, planned well in advance of the service. The testifier will perhaps give the testimony in writing to the leader, who will know exactly where it might fit in the worship service, and there is rarely more than one such testimony on a particular day.

I wouldn't offer an opinion as to which of these is better—although, as friends have pointed out to me, I do have an opinion.

However, even though I imagine we all can think of pros and cons for each, and we all probably have our own opinion about which side should win if it were to come to a vote, I suspect that where the testimony is concerned it might not matter when or where it happens.

What does matter is that there is a true testimony of God's work in our lives and that our children are exposed to it.

Come to think of it, it also matters—and matters a great deal—what God thinks about the testimony. He probably *does* have an opinion.

After all, it was his idea to begin with.

THINKING ABOUT CHAPTER FOUR

SELF DISCOVERY QUESTIONS:

1. Do you remember testimonies that helped you?

2. Have you ever shared your own story/stories about God's goodness in your life?

3. If you have, why did you?

4. If you haven't, why not?

KEEPERS' PRAYER:

Dear Father,

Thank you for the stories I've heard. May I always value their message, and may they always fulfill their purpose in my life.

CHAPTER FIVE

~

The Purpose of
the Testimony

*"The testimony of the Lord is sure,
making wise the simple."*

~Psalm 19:7

~5~

IN THINKING BACK over the hundreds or, perhaps more accurately, thousands of testimonies I have heard over several decades of church life, I have concluded we sometimes—not always, but sometimes—lose sight of why we are to testify.

The testimony has a very specific purpose and it is not to earn points with God. If we, as speakers or hearers, keep its true purpose in the forefront of our mind, it will affect how we share and even how we receive the testimony.

I'm sure we're well aware that the purpose of the testimony has nothing to do with collecting Heavenly Brownie points. But neither is its purpose merely to inform the hearer about God, nor to convince of his existence, nor even to confirm his power. As important as each of these is, the testimony has a purpose that goes way beyond any of them.

In my first book, *What's in a Name*, there is a chapter in which I write about an important aspect of one's name: reputation. There we can see if not the whole purpose then, at least, a significant part of the purpose God had in mind for the testimony. Here's a quote from that chapter:

> God knew, long before our twenty-first century marketers and publicists, that being known and being positively perceived is important. Psalm 76:1 says, "in Judah God is known: his name is great in Israel." When

God truly is known and his character and works reported accurately, then his name, his reputation, is *very* great.

God gave explicit instructions to the children of Israel to ensure his reputation would continue to be known and that he would be represented accurately in the earth. In Psalm 78, we see the children of Israel were to pass on to their children the reputation of God by telling them about his mighty acts toward his people. We also see the reason they were to do it.

> *"We will not hide them from our children, shewing to the generation to come the praises of the Lord, and his strength, and his wonderful works that he hath done. For he established a testimony in Jacob, and appointed a law in Israel, which he commanded our fathers, that they should make them known to their children: That the generation to come might know them, even the children which should be born; who should arise and declare them to their children:* **That they might set their hope in God, and not forget the works of God and keep his commandments"** *(Psalm 78: 4-7).*

There we have a three-fold reason for the testimony. If that was its stated purpose back then, we can safely assume it still is since there is no suggestion—at least none that I know of—that God's desire has changed.

Clearly, every testimony from that day until this has had these three purposes:

1. The hearers would remember God's works.

2. They would set their hope in him.

3. They would be faithful to walk in his commandments, or his ways, all of which were given for the benefit of his children.

That's quite a response to a testimony! It certainly would be evidence of the simple made wise (Psalm 19:7).

That's the intended response to the testimony, but has it been the response to the testimonies we've heard?

Probably not.

Certainly, I've heard stirring testimonies I've carried with me for years, testimonies that have inspired me to hope in God. I have also—as have you, I imagine—heard testimonies that didn't seem to be testimonies about God as much as a litany of trials and troubles faced of late or even, alas, throughout life. Of course, there followed an assertion that, through it all, God had been faithful or that, in spite of it all, the testifier had remained faithful to God.

Not that it's a bad thing. It's good to remain faithful in trial, and its telling does provide a good example to follow. In fact, to a great degree we can look at the ability to be patient and faithful to God in the midst of trouble as a gift, an empowerment from God himself. If that is the case—as I'm pretty sure it is, and as the testifiers no doubt wanted to communicate—then certainly we should be thankful for that gift.

But somehow those weren't the testimonies that caused me to set my hope in God. Instead of focusing on God, those stories—with no deliberate intent by the testifier, I'm sure—focused on how patient the faithful one had been. That usually resulted in my admiration of the faithful but, more often than not, also brought on considerable angst about my own poor performance, actual or anticipated. I was sure I would never be that good a Christian.

Challenging though they may have been, those stories rarely caused me to delight in or even think about the character and works of God. The testimonies that kept my eyes on God were those in which God's name was unmistakably the one being enhanced. Thankfully, I heard lots of those.

As indicated earlier, I do not want to suggest that the other testimonies were deliberately enhancing someone else's reputation. I'm sure they weren't; that was just how I heard them. But still, the truly encouraging testimonies were those which clearly showed God's goodness and faithfulness. They were the stories in which the resolution—even if it was not the one the testifier originally wanted—was one which only

God could bring about and which plainly showed his goodness and his faithfulness to keep his word.

Because our eyes and hearts are captured by the hero of any story we hear, God should be the obvious hero in every testimony.

THINKING ABOUT CHAPTER FIVE

SELF DISCOVERY QUESTIONS:

1. Have the testimonies you've heard enhanced God's reputation in your mind?

2. Have the testimonies you've heard made you wiser?

3. Have the testimonies you've heard caused you to hope in God?

4. Have the testimonies you've shared done any of those for someone else?

KEEPERS' PRAYER:

Dear Lord,
  Help me to tell your stories well.

CHAPTER SIX

~

The Power of
the Testimony

"And I fell at his feet to worship him. And he said unto me, see thou do it not: I am thy fellow servant, and of thy brethren that have the testimony of Jesus: worship God, for the testimony of Jesus is the spirit of prophecy."

~Revelation 19:10

~6~

REVELATION 19:10 MAKES A STATEMENT that for years was a complete mystery to me. It says the testimony of Jesus is the spirit of prophecy.

That scripture from the book of Revelation indicates that the story of Jesus has a prophetic aspect. Every time the story of Jesus is told—that he died for the sins of the world—it prophesies something to the hearer that gives hope. It calls the hearer to believe the promise of the gospel—the good news of Jesus' birth, death, and resurrection for our redemption—and to make a choice which will affect his or her destiny eternally. Its purpose is always the same: to inspire hope which initiates action.

When I found out what Revelation 19:10 meant[1], I finally understood why I so enjoyed the testimonies of the older members of the congregation all those years ago. I'm sure I didn't recognize it back then, but what I actually loved about their testimonies was their prophecy. Their stories told me that whosoever will believe on the Lord Jesus Christ and confess him as Lord can have a life blessed by God's presence—that anyone can expect God to be faithful and

---

[1] I recommend a tape series entitled *Healing: Our Neglected Birthright* by Pastor Bill Johnson of Bethel Church in Redding, California.

true for a lifetime and beyond. Even as a child I needed the hope offered by that prophecy.

In the last chapter, I wrote that God should be the hero of every testimony. Think of our favorite heroes, either real life or fictional. Hasn't every hero of every story we've ever loved brought hope to the hopeless?

Think of the courageous and determined woman who rescued a child from the lonely life of a deaf-mute; or those valiant ones who did what they could to help a race of people targeted for extinction; or the many ordinary heroes who by way of an underground railroad set free frightened and desperate slaves a handful at a time; or the young marine who risked his life to rescue wounded workers trapped in the rubble of fallen twin towers on September 11, 2001.

Don't we love stories like theirs? They surely were the Bravehearts of their time and place, and we never tire of hearing about them. We love heroes.

In the same way, the testimony in which God is the hero, as he is in the testimony of Jesus, is the one that we love and carry with us for a lifetime. We do so, not just because it's a great story and we love heroes, but because it has within it the spirit of prophecy which is, and always has been, the intended and actual power of any testimony.

If we look back to when God instructed Moses to celebrate feast days, we will see it was so his people would, as the central focus of the celebration, continually remember his works and commemorate his faithfulness. We've already seen why he wanted them to do that—so they would hope in him and walk in his ways.

Interestingly, those feasts don't just chronicle something God did in the past. As New Testament believers, we can clearly see that each of them also prophesied something God was going to do in the future through the first or second coming of Jesus. That prophecy still gives hope which inspires the believer to action: to purify his heart (1 John 3:3).

It seems that hope always results in action of some sort. We see it in the gospels. How often have we read there about people who heard of Jesus' fame and came rushing to him to hear his gracious words and receive their sick healed? They came because the stories they heard had become prophecies to them. Just listen:

- "If I can just get to him, things will change. If I can touch his clothes, then ..."

- "If he will just come and touch my daughter, then she ..."

- "If he just says the word, then my servant ..."

Because of someone's stories, a very sick and, no doubt, exhausted woman found hope that motivated her to push through a throng just to touch Jesus' clothes; a man heard stories that gave him the courage to beg that Jesus come to his house and lay hands on his dying daughter; and a soldier understood Jesus' authority and said, "Don't come! Just say the word. Your word is enough."

Something in the stories they heard did that for them; it gave them that kind of hope.

Prophecy—even prophecy born of the testimony—creates an atmosphere where impossibilities become possible and the hearer is motivated to act.

It follows, therefore, that whenever we hear a story, a testimony, about Jesus' work in the life of another, it should create in us an expectation—a hope of something good—which spurs us to action, even if that action is simply to obey the direction: "Be still and know that I am God" (Psalm 46:10).

Jesus lived those stories and many more as he walked with his disciples through the streets of Capernaum, along the shores of the Galilee, and over the hills round about Jerusalem. The effect those stories had on multitudes of people of that day is obvious, but the testimony had the same effect long before then. We've seen that when Psalm 78—which we read earlier—was written, the psalmist knew that the power of the testimony was in its forward looking property.

When Jacob told his children about all God had done, it was not only that they should know God's power and might. Such knowledge alone would have been an important piece of information for the Israelites to have, but it is clear that in God's eyes it wasn't enough that they should just know more about him. He had something else in mind, something very important to him because it was necessary to the fulfillment of his good purposes on the planet. It was important to God that the Israelites not only know what he had done in the past but that they should also expect he would do the same for them in their present and their future.

The reason they could expect that—or at least one reason for it—is that the covenant God made with Abraham was not just for Abraham but also for his children's children in their generation. God wanted them all to look to the future with confidence in their covenant.

No end in sight.

They had covenant promises and they had testimonies. The testimony was to show Jacob's children that God—the almighty God, maker of Heaven and earth—was also the faithful God who kept his covenant.

Millennia later, nothing has changed. Remember how in those testimony services years ago the senior saints talked about God's goodness and faithfulness? Their stories created an expectation in me—a hope that, in my life, too, he would be faithful to his covenant if I would learn to walk with him.

The power of a testimony has always been in its prophecy, and it still is. In our day, the testimony has the same purpose and power as it did back then.

That's why the testimony of Jesus has met with such opposition in a world attempting to become increasingly secular. As I'm writing this we've just finished another Christmas season. More than any other year there seemed to be a definite push this year to remove the name of Jesus from the celebration. Outside of bookstores devoted to Christian material one was hard put to find Christmas cards with any reference to the blessed event for which the season was meant to be celebrated.

Ostensibly, the reason for this crusade is sensitivity to people of other faiths with whom we share our multicultural nation. That sounds reasonable and kind and, of course, unquestionably Canadian. However, although no true Christian, Canadian or otherwise, would consider it right to be unkind to people of other faiths or demand that the words Ramadan or Hanukah be banished from our public vocabulary, no true Christian will be content to celebrate Christmas as a merely secular holiday.

The attempt to turn Christmas into a purely secular event is, undoubtedly, the modern version of an ancient endeavor, the annihilation of the testimony. Since the celebration of Christmas as the birthday of the Savior is part of keeping the testimony, to let it go in favor of political correctness is to cooperate with the attack.

However, sadly, it is not only in the world at large that the testimony of Jesus has suffered attack. A more subtle assault has been made on our own hearts and minds, personally and collectively. That devious onslaught was perhaps the greatest cause of the demise of the testimony service in our churches, in the workplace, or even socially over coffee with fellow believers.

I've seen the result of this assault in the faces of good, God-fearing, God-loving, God-worshiping Christians. I've seen it in churches as congregants sat listening to the rare testimony given from the pulpit, and in small groups as believers listened to others share their experiences with God. It has even shown up in coffee shops as someone dared to bring the name of Jesus and the goodness of God into a conversation as if they have any bearing on everyday life.

What I've seen in their faces is something I have felt myself, and which, thankfully, I can guard against now that I am aware. It is by no means doubt or unbelief. Most of us do believe that God can do all they say he's done, and we, by and large, believe that God actually has done it. There's no unbelief in God or in the testifier.

There's no unbelief, but neither is there hope. It is something very different from hope.

Thank God it isn't always there, but it is there often enough to be addressed in a book about keeping the testimony.

THINKING ABOUT CHAPTER SIX

SELF DISCOVERY QUESTIONS:

1. How do you feel about the idea that your testimonies are/should be prophetic?

2. Does it make you uncomfortable about sharing them? Why? Why not?

3. Would you like your hearers to get hope from your testimonies?

KEEPERS' PRAYER:

Father,

Please help me see when I'm hiding the testimony or letting it go in favor of political correctness. Help me see if I'm letting it go for any other reason.

CHAPTER SEVEN

~

The Wounds of
the Attack

*"I will speak of Thy testimonies before kings
and will not be ashamed."*

~Psalm 119:46

~7~

I REMEMBER SITTING one day in a friend's home sipping tea while she shared about the financial trouble she and her husband were in. It seemed they could never get ahead of the bills and almost always had too much month left at the end of the money. They had already moved several times in order to lower expenses, and she was tired of it.

In an attempt to kick-start her apparently flagging hope in God's care, I told her the stories about how God had provided for my family and me while we were in Texas.

They were great stories, and I often deliberately recalled them when I needed to encourage myself in challenging times. Unfortunately, they didn't have the same effect on her. Somewhere in the middle of one of them I saw her eyes darken. I should have stopped right then and let her talk, but I didn't. Later, in sorry hindsight, I could see I hadn't done a good job of sharing the testimony because by the time I finished she had pretty much shut down and dropped the subject. We talked, instead, about the paint on the walls of their new apartment.

What could possibly be found in the eyes of a Christian as she hears stories about what her Father has done? There should only be good things like hope and, yes, even satisfaction of a sort—the kind of satisfaction any child might have at seeing her father do something wonderful. Yet, sometimes there is something else. There is a mixture of dark elements, several of which were in my friend's eyes that day.

The mix can change from time to time and from person to person but the result is the same wherever they are present: The testimony has lost its power.

Those dark elements of the mix are not spoken of here in any order of importance or chronology. They are just there, in the eyes and hearts of too many followers of Jesus, and they are there without their consent. In fact, the good hearts of the hearers would be ashamed to recognize such unlovely attitudes in themselves.

One very dark and painful element is jealousy. That may sound like an unkind accusation but I don't mean it to be either unkind or accusatory. The jealousy is quite natural. It's the kind of jealousy one child would feel if a beloved father or mother were to especially favor another of their children over the one. Sibling rivalry for a parent's affection or attention is common.

You may be thinking that even though we know such rivalry happens all too often within families, most often the inequity which causes it happens only in the mind of the child, not in actuality.

I believe you are right.

You may also be thinking that everyone knows God loves us all the same. After all, "God so loved the world" (John 3:16), not just a few special ones. The Bible also tells us God is no respecter of persons (see Colossians 3:25). That means he treats us all the same, right?

Right, again.

But that's not what the hearer is thinking. It may be what his reason tells him but, if he's going through a difficult time and if he can't find the prophecy in the testimony he's hearing, it's not what his heart tells him. If he doesn't hear prophecy, his heart tells him another is beloved and he is not.

I think that is what my friend heard in my inept attempt to encourage her. Somehow, her heart heard that God loved my family more than he did hers—or maybe, simply, that I believed he did for some reason. Either thought would have hurt and would have influenced negatively her ability to receive my testimony. It is only natural that, born of the lie that says another is preferred, the hurt of rejection eventually appears.

It hurts to think we're not loved as much as another, especially when every fiber of our being says two children in the same family should be equally loved. Even though one child may be enjoyed more than another because of differences in personality, instinct screams that equity of love and favor in families is right and good, and that inequity is wrong, unfair, and perhaps even unnatural. The perceived unfairness and sense of rejection give birth, as we would expect, to yet another of the dark elements: resentment.

So there it is: The spiritual family operating much like a natural family. Whether or not the motivation for the testimony is right, we sometimes resent the testifier—if not for experiencing the story, then, at least, for telling it. We might have been happy to hear the story in better times when things were going well in our own lives, but now we think it unkind for the testifier to stand there and talk about how he has been favored by God and, in doing so, make us feel somehow less than favored. In our pain, we wonder why anyone would do that. Why make someone else feel badly? Why not be more sensitive to the feelings of others? Why not just experience your blessings privately and worship privately and leave the rest of us to do the same?

Doesn't that echo the reason for the politically correct holiday with which some would have us replace Christmas? I guess the perpetrator of the attack has limited weapons.

Any true Christian will not be at all surprised at the final element of the dark mixture. Always and at last, shame raises its cruel banner and claims its place. We are ashamed we feel rejection, mortified that we are jealous, disgusted by our resentment. None of us want to feel those things. We know we should be rejoicing with those who rejoice and praising God along with them but we aren't. Not really.

We just smile and maybe even clap, if that's the custom of the church, and say, "Praise the Lord!"

And then we carry on as before.

Oh yes, there's our mental note to never make someone else feel the way we have been made to feel. *We'll* be more thoughtful and considerate. *We'll* keep our testimonies to ourselves.

And, interestingly enough, that's exactly what the testifier often decides. After all, he's seen the eyes looking back at him.

As a result, the sharing of the testimony becomes a rare event and in some places stops altogether. And so does the prophecy.

The assault has been effective.

THINKING ABOUT CHAPTER SEVEN

SELF DISCOVERY QUESTIONS:

1. Have you ever felt jealousy, resentment, or shame as you've listened to someone else's testimony?

2. Have you ever seen those responses in someone else as you've told your own stories?

3. If the answer to either of those questions was "Yes," what effect did it have on you?

KEEPERS' PRAYER:

Father,

Thank you for knowing me completely and yet loving me absolutely. Thank you for teaching me patiently. Help me to hear the testimonies well.

CHAPTER EIGHT

~

The Source of the Attack

*"Be not therefore ashamed of the testimony of our Lord,
nor of me his prisoner:
but be thou a partaker of the afflictions of the gospel
according to the power of God."*

~2 Timothy 1:8

~8~

THE PURPOSE OF THE ATTACK has always been the same: Somehow stop the telling and, in doing so, stop the prophecy.

The source also has been the same.

In the Old Testament, who was behind the killing of the prophets? Who was affecting the crazed mind of King Saul when he was hot on the trail of David, that most effective teller of God's stories? Who lopped off the head of John the Baptist to shut him up? Who told Peter and John to stop talking about Jesus and refrain from teaching in his name? And who tried to stop the Word made flesh by tempting him to change his path?

It was the same source.

The source, the spirit of anti-Christ, is still here and still actively trying to kill the testimony.

To clearly visualize the whole point of the attack, imagine a world—your world—if there were no testimony. Imagine if you'd never heard of the God of Abraham, Isaac, and Jacob. Think of what your world would look like if you'd never heard the story of Jesus. What would life be like if you'd never heard about someone who not only loves you but has the power and desire to be the strength of your life and your hope of life after this one?

Dr James Kennedy and Jerry Newcombe have written a book about what our world would be like today if Jesus had never been born, entitled, appropriately, *What If Jesus Had Never Been Born?* I imagine our world would look much the same as they describe if the spirit of anti-Christ had been able to wipe out the testimony of Jesus' life.

At the very least, you and I would not be hoping in God.

In *What's in a Name*, I write about the testimony in this way:

> We may be aware of God's love and mercy but we still could never have faith for the new birth if he hadn't said it was available to all who would believe. Neither could we have faith for salvation if we didn't *know* what he said about it. We easily recognize that fact as the reason for the Great Commission: Go ye into all the world and preach the gospel. Apparently an individual's knowledge of the promise of salvation is crucial to its fulfillment in his or her life.

There it is. To sum it up simply, the knowledge of the promise is necessary. And the knowledge of God's faithfulness is just as necessary. That's what the testimony is all about. The true testimony tells not only the promise, but also God's faithfulness to fulfill the promise. That's what creates the prophecy and the hope.

I can hear someone reading this and saying, "But I hadn't read any promises before I came to Jesus. I didn't know anything. I was a Biblical illiterate!" Actually, even though many testimonies of salvation start that same way, they really do begin with a promise even though sometimes the promise is only recognized in hindsight.

I know that needs some explanation. These next couple of stories might help clarify what I'm trying to say.

I once heard a story about a missionary who went to the northern part of Russia to minister to nomadic Eskimo tribes. No other missionary had been there—at least, not in recent history. When he arrived, he spoke with the help of an interpreter to a man who had come out from the village to greet them. The missionary, through the interpreter, told him they had come to tell the people of the village about the God who had created the earth, and about his son, Jesus. The man's eyes misted. His wrinkled face beamed and he offered a broken-toothed grin as he replied, "At last! I knew someone would come to tell me."

Apparently, this man had looked at the stars and the vast land of ice and snow in which he lived, and he knew someone must have created it all. No one had told him about God, but the heavens had declared his existence, just as Psalm 19 says. Somehow, the faithfulness of the sunrises and sunsets testified to him of the faithfulness of their Creator. Nature prophesied to him and created the hope that its Creator was someone he could know. He prayed and asked this unknown God to send someone who would teach him. And God did.

Today I chatted with a young lady about her own experience of salvation. We both were amazed as we recognized the part an unspoken promise played in her coming to faith in Christ. She had first heard the promise as she watched her younger sister, a devout Christian who was always peaceful and happy. My friend's life was neither peaceful nor happy. Without a word spoken, her sister's life testified to her and told of a better life that she, too, could have if she would put her faith in Jesus and let him be Lord of her life.

That was the promise she believed and acted on. Her sister's life prophesied a future that gave her hope. She acted on that hope and has found the peace she was looking for, even in the midst of a challenging world.

Whether read, heard, or seen, and whether intellectually understood or gut-felt, there will always be some form of promise that prophesies hope.

And no matter what the form of the promise, our enemy, the diabolical source of the assault, is against it. He is against both the promise and the hope it gives. He wants to destroy them both because they are necessary for the outcomes God wants to see on the earth, and because where they remain intact they eventually bring glory to the God who gave them.

It's that simple and that profound.

The thief comes not but for to steal, kill, and destroy (John 10:10).

He comes to steal the promise, kill the hope, and destroy the glory.

THINKING ABOUT CHAPTER EIGHT

SELF DISCOVERY QUESTIONS:

1. Has the perpetrator of the attacks mentioned in this chapter ever attacked you?

2. If so, how?

3. Did you fight back?

4. If so, how?

KEEPERS' PRAYER:

Dear Father,

Help me never again to lose sight of your faithfulness. Help me never to lose hope in you. Help me never to cooperate with the attacker. May I never again silence the testimonies.

CHAPTER NINE

~

Promises That Prophesy

"Thy testimonies also are my delight and my counselors."

~Psalm 119:24

~9~

PROPHECY IS ALL ABOUT HOPE.

The prophecy I'm talking about is not the description of future events that we see through the Old and New Testaments. Neither am I talking about the gift of the Spirit that Paul teaches about in his first letter to the Corinthians, where believers prophesy to the church body, nor even the personal prophetic word given to individuals through a modern day prophet. Many of us go through our whole lives and never receive such a word.

I'm talking about the prophecy evident throughout the Bible in its records of God's dealings with man. In the history they give we are to find God's character and covenant and his ways, and *these* are prophetic.

It's important to remember that not everything recorded in the Bible expresses God's will. Many things that happened were in opposition to God's will, but even as we see his response to these we can see God's righteous ways and his heart for his people. All of these—God's character, his will, and his righteous ways—are supposed to create hope in us. They are supposed to create a vision and expectation of good which comes from the hand of the giver of all good gifts.

So it is with our stories. They are to show the same, and do the same.

But what might steal the testimony's prophetic power? What is the attack that causes the wounds we see in the eyes of the faithful?

It is simply this. When the testimony is either given or heard from the perspective of merely recalling an event, rather than showing God's character as evidenced by his actions and his faithfulness to do what he has said he will do, it is just history. The past, itself, is not an accurate predictor of the future, and we know it.

Because of that, as we listen to stories about what God has done for others or even read about them in the Bible, these stories fall at our feet, useless and unfruitful, if we cannot hear in them something about God that tells us how he will act in the future and in *our* lives.

Somewhere along the way, the source of the attack—the thief—has stolen the realization that God's actions on behalf of one person show his will and his heart for us all. We've forgotten that if he has ever forgiven anyone, he will forgive each of us. If he has ever provided for anyone, he will provide for any of us. If he has ever answered anyone's prayer—certainly, prayer based on his promises[2]—he wants to do the same for all.

I can feel someone squirming in discomfort at what I've just said. I hear, "How can we know that?"

I understand both the discomfort and the question because experience shouts loudly that what I've said is not true. Experience says that many prayers aren't answered, or if they were the answer was "No!" My experience has said that, and so has yours.

But experience alone doesn't reveal God to us. He does.

---

[2] For example, if we don't know what God's will is in a particular situation, such as which job should be ours, then simply praying for his will to be done would be appropriate. In that situation we can pray that he will provide our need, a job in this case, and confidently expect that he will provide the very best one, based on his promise in Philippians 4:19.

We can know these things *are* true because, if it is *not* the case, God would never have said the testimony is to give reason for hope.

In fact, if it is not the case, any stories we hear about God will only have the effect of showing God's existence and power. They won't show his goodness, faithfulness, mercy, and kindness. They will tell about something that happened once, twice, or no matter how many times, but won't prophesy anyone's future.

Where there is no prediction of future good, there is no hope. Not even in the testimony.

But we've already seen that the testimony is supposed to carry with it future-predicting, hope-creating prophecy.

Think about it: We would quickly chastise someone who gave his own testimony of salvation by faith in Jesus but then said it might not be available to all who would receive the promise. What would be the point of the testimony in that case except to brag about one's good fortune and to torment the unfortunate hearer for whom the good may be unavailable?

I know it sounds preposterous, and so it is.

It would have been just as preposterous for Jacob's children to have been told the stories of what God had done for their ancestors but also have been told such favor might not be available to them. We know it didn't happen that way. The stories were always told in a way that gave evidence of God's faithfulness to do what he said he would do. They also confirmed that his faithfulness would always remain the same. He would always do what he said he would do if his covenant partners, the Israelites, would walk in his ways.

Therein they found their hope.

Their hope was in the fact that the covenant promises remained sure—that is, their availability was secure—to all who would put their hope in, and follow after, the God who gave them.

THINKING ABOUT CHAPTER NINE

SELF DISCOVERY QUESTIONS:

1. Have you ever thought of testimonies as merely stories that prove God's existence?

2. Have you thought about the testimony as a carrier of hope for you?

3. Have you ever listened and deliberately looked for the hope in them?

4. When you tell your stories, do you see them as hope-builders?

KEEPERS' PRAYER:

Father,

Help me to remember whose story I'm telling and why I'm telling it. May my stories bring honor to your great name and give encouragement to those who hear them.

CHAPTER TEN

~

The Plan

*"I have rejoiced in the way of Thy testimonies,
as much as in all riches."*

~Psalm 119:14

~10~

THAT'S WHERE they found their hope, and that's where we find ours.

I can hear someone saying "Now there's a daunting thought! Surely our hope is not in our ability to walk in God's ways. If that's the case, then I am truly hopeless. I'm not sure I even know all of God's ways."

Did this picture just flash in your mind, as it did in mine, of poor frustrated Christian trying to run the maze before him, failing in his attempt to clear the obstacles and pitfalls on his path, and knowing he's on his own in this struggle unless he gets everything right?

Quickly, delete the picture!

Actually, I'd be willing to bet you have already done so. I'm sure most of us know more about, and have experienced more of, God's grace and loving kindness than that picture would suggest. We know they have nothing to do with our performance. They are not dependent on our ability to live perfectly, getting it right all the time. Even in looking back at the Israelites' journeys and those of the early apostles, we clearly see it's not the perfection of the walk but rather the direction of the walk and, certainly, the Companion on the walk that counts.

However, knowing that—and maybe even *because* we know that—we still might have difficulty figuring out just what is required of us, if anything, on this walk with God.

What are God's ways, anyway? They might seem illusive, changing with time as the norms of our denominations change; but, surely, if we search we can find those ways that are, like God, both unchangeable and knowable.

If we think about it for a while, we'll recognize that the phrase "God's ways" can have several meanings. If we consider each of them, we might get a clearer picture of what he wants us to walk in.

JESUS: THE WAY

Firstly, the most basic of God's ways we give testament to and which clearly shows his character of love and mercy is found in the words of Jesus written in the Gospel of John: "I am the way, the truth and the life. No man comes unto the Father except by me (John 14:6). " This way is prerequisite to living a life of experiential knowledge of God.

While anyone can live a good life based on Godly principles, and will, no doubt, receive good fruit from doing so, no one can receive eternal life and live the life God has destined without first accepting Jesus as savior. That step is the beginning of any life that fulfills the destiny God has planned. It is the first step in walking in God's ways.

Still, it is just the beginning of the walk. While it is, thankfully, true that anyone can call on Jesus on their deathbed and receive eternal life at that very moment, it is just as true that anyone can receive Jesus as savior early in life and still neglect to walk with him in such a way that results in God's plan and purpose being established in his life.

In either case, God's *perfect* plan for the life of a Christian remains the same: Know God's will, hope in him, and walk in his ways, as we mentioned in Chapter 5.

PATHS TO CHOOSE

Secondly, God's ways can refer to the paths in which God leads man. We're told that God showed his ways to Moses and his acts to the children of Israel. We know that Moses had a close walking relationship with God—maybe because of his calling or because of his heart's desire and willingness to seek God and obey him. Because of that relationship, Moses received direction from God about the way to take on the journey, and knew what God expected of him and what moved God (see Exodus 32) even though he didn't have the written record of God's ways and of his will that we have.

The children of Israel, on the other hand, like many today, may have seen what God did but they didn't know his ways. I wouldn't presume to suggest why they didn't, although their refusal to come near the mountain to hear his voice may tell us something about it (see Deuteronomy 5:24-27). No matter what the reason, the account of their journey does imply that God has ways of doing things—ways of dealing with man, and ways of leading him—and that we can actually learn what they are and walk in them.

GOD'S ACTIONS

The phrase "God's ways" might also refer to those actions which are the natural outflow of God's character. God is holy, just, loving, merciful, gracious, kind, and faithful; we could go on. Certainly, knowing these attributes, we can expect his actions to be reflective of them. Because of God's character, he behaves in certain predictable ways, and though it may be difficult for us to understand how he can be holy, just, merciful, and kind all at the same time, an understanding of his works will show us that he is.

WISDOM PRINCIPLES

The last use of the phrase we will consider here, and one which is almost inseparable from the ones previously mentioned, refers to living a lifestyle which reflects God's wisdom. Just as there are principles involving God's dealings with man, there are also ways or principles in which we are to respond to God and by which we are to govern our relationships on this earth in a manner that will bring blessing. It is our responsibility to discover specific principles or directions and walk in them. In every step of the way, the power and responsibility to choose is ours.

There is wisdom and direction in all of God's ways. For example, none of us would think we could fulfill our destiny—establishing God's plan *for* our lives and receiving that which is God's will *in* our lives—by walking in our own ways of hate and recrimination or even of lovelessness and self-serving behavior. It doesn't seem probable, does it? It simply makes sense that walking in his ways of love and grace and mercy will be more likely to help us keep our feet to his path.

Other examples of God's wisdom principles come to mind:

1. "As you stand praying, forgive."

2. "Do unto others as you would have them do unto you."

3. "Give and it shall be given unto you."

4. "No man can serve two masters."

Of course, these are just examples of what I'm talking about; there are many, many more. We should never be at a loss for wisdom.

Are we beginning to see that God's ways are knowable?

Paul the apostle, in his letter to the Colossians in which he tells them about a prayer he prays for them constantly, seems to indicate we can know God's will and therefore know the ways in which we are to walk. In Paul's prayer we also see the effect of walking in God's ways.

"For this cause we also, since the day we heard it [your love in the spirit] do not cease to pray for you, and to desire that you might be filled with the knowledge of His will in all wisdom and spiritual understanding; that you might walk worthy of the Lord unto all pleasing, being fruitful in every good work, and increasing in the knowledge of God, strengthened with all might according to His glorious power, unto all patience and long suffering, with joyfulness; giving thanks to the Father, which made us meet [qualified] to be partakers of the inheritance of the saints in light" *(Colossians 1:9-12).*

Paul's prayer was for people who were already believers. That suggests to me that one can be a believer but still not be filled with knowledge of God and his will. It also clearly suggests that if we know God's will and have his wisdom and understanding they will help us to walk worthy of him, partaking of our inheritance and being fruitful in every good work, strengthened with the might which comes from his power, and filled with patience, thankfulness, and joy. In this one prayer we can hear echoed the same reason for the testimony referred to in Psalm 78.

*"We will not hide them from our children, **shewing to the generation to come the praises of the Lord, and his strength, and his wonderful works that he hath done.** For he established a testimony in Jacob, and appointed a law in Israel, which he commanded our fathers, that they should make them known to their children: That the generation to come might know them, even the children which should be born; who should arise and declare them to their children: **That they might set their hope in God, and not forget the works of God and keep his commandments"** (Psalm 78: 4-7).*

There it is again. The purpose of the testimony is that we might know, hope, and walk. It almost seems the knowing and hoping are prerequisites of our successful walking in his ways. Perhaps if we don't know, we won't hope; and if we have no hope, we won't walk.

God wants us to know him, know his will, hope in him, and walk with him. Many scriptures indicate that God has a plan for good and not evil, to give us a future and a hope; they also show us that the fulfillment of the plan is connected to our choices.

That is probably why we parents focus so much of our children's training on living righteously and making right choices. We want our children to make good choices and, in so doing, have a good, hope-filled future.

But that future doesn't come from merely obeying laws or principles written millennia ago. It comes from a vital relationship—one which requires intimate knowledge.

The successful working out of God's good plan starts with knowing him.

That may be why the children of Israel spent so much time in the wilderness. Remember, they came right up to the Promised Land and, no doubt, could have gone in and taken it, but when the spies came back with two different synopses of the situation, they caved in.

You know how the song goes: "Twelve spies went to spy in Canaan. Ten were bad; two were good." The good ones said, "The land flows with milk and honey and we are well able to take it!" The ten bad spies said, "There are giants who will crush us like spiders under their feet!"

The Israelites had the right to choose whom they would believe, and they believed the spies who brought the bad report. After all, there actually were huge giants in the land! The children of Israel were afraid to face the giants, so they refused to go in and take the land promised to them. Since they refused to go in, God had to take them on a circuitous route.

There were possibly two reasons for that detour. The first reason was no doubt so that the generation who refused to go in would pass away. God wouldn't force them to go in against their wishes. Maybe he knew that with fear dictating their actions they couldn't take the land, anyway, so they *and* their children would have been slaughtered by the giants.

The second reason he took them through the desert may have been so he could help the rest of them get to know him better. Clearly, they didn't know their God yet—most of them anyway. Because of that lack of true knowledge of God, they didn't believe he'd be with them and give them good success. As a result, they were filled with fear at what they saw ahead of them. His people had lived in slavery for four hundred years and now they had to learn how to live free. God would teach them but he could only do that if they had a living, walking, vital relationship with him. Maybe then they would believe what he said, hope in him, and walk in his ways. Maybe then they would take their land.

So what does all of that have to do with us and our story telling?

Just this: We've seen that the testimony is to give hope. Hope is why the most effective testimony will not just show God's existence and power but will also illustrate his character, his will, and his ways.

However, even though the strongest basis for hope is an intimate, experiential knowledge of God which will be developed over time, God still has the novice covered. Our stories have an effect because the Holy Spirit, teacher of the church and the revealer of truth, gets involved in the telling and hearing of the testimony, and even someone who hasn't yet had time to develop his own relationship with God will find hope in the testimony. As the Holy Spirit reveals the truth carried by our words, our hearers will respond to the hope they hear and will begin their own journey of faith.

We each have a lovingly designed journey, but it is our understanding of and walking in God's ways that bring us to the expected end we hear about in Jeremiah 29:11, "For I know the thoughts I think toward you says the Lord, thoughts of peace, and not of evil, to give you an expected end."

Even though God is talking there to the children of Israel, we know he has the same thoughts toward each of us, the people of the New Covenant. I'm sure you can remember the words of Jesus, "I am come that they might have life, and that they might have it more abundantly" (John 10:10).

We are all included in the word "they," but not everyone takes advantage of what he came to give. Something is required of us—something we can do. As we do it, we receive that life abundantly.

The whole point of telling the stories is so our listeners will hear God's praises, know his will, hope in him, and walk with him, confident in the knowledge of his ways, enjoying the inheritance he provided, being fruitful in every good work, slaying giants, and taking their own promised land.

And—can you see it?—another testimony is born which brings praise to his name.

It's a great plan!

THINKING ABOUT CHAPTER TEN

SELF DISCOVERY QUESTIONS:

1. Do you feel you know God's ways?

2. Have you ever thought you couldn't possibly know God's ways?

3. Have you ever searched specifically to find out what God's ways are?

KEEPERS' PRAYER:

Help me to know your ways, Lord. Help me to walk with you.

CHAPTER ELEVEN

~

The Problem

"Many are my persecutors and mine enemies;
yet I do not decline from thy testimonies."

~Psalm 119:157

~11~

THERE IN SIMPLIFIED FORM we have the plan: Hear the good news, believe the good news, and hope in God. Expect him to do what he says, and do what he tells you.

Think about it: After we believe on the Lord Jesus Christ, we don't constantly worry about whether or not we are going to be good enough to go to Heaven when we die, do we?

Not at all!

Instead, we trust in Jesus and believe in what he did for us. We confess with our mouth that he is our Savior and Lord, just as he said he would be. We begin there and walk with him on this earth, following him all the way to our heavenly home. We have received the wonderful promise that "He that believeth on me hath everlasting life" (John 6:47), and it has become the basis of our blessed hope.

Of course, that's what every promise is meant to do, bring hope. So you can imagine my shock when I heard a Christian leader, a good man, say that the words, "Believe on the Lord Jesus Christ and thou shalt be saved," spoken by Paul and Silas to the keeper of the prison at Thyatira (see Acts 16:31), contain the only promise God guarantees to fulfill.

It probably sounds shocking to you, too, but if you think about it for a minute you may understand why he said it, and why that thought has actually become an enemy to the keeping of the testimony.

I believe the reason he said it and the reason many of us believe it—or if we don't actually believe it, we still live as though it's true—is this: When we see all the sadness and suffering, the immeasurable heartaches, innumerable atrocities, and epic natural disasters in the world, and when we see personal tragedies, abuses, losses, and suffering in the lives of Christians everywhere, it appears that there are a lot of unfulfilled promises. So, to that gentleman, as to many others among us, it made sense that God guarantees only one promise.

Now think of what that thought does to the hearer of any testimony.

Imagine New Christian rising from his knees at the altar with tears of joy on his face. He has just heard what Jesus did for him. He has heard and believed the promise that eternal life will be given to all who believe the good news and receive Jesus as Savior and Lord. He has prayed and received, with overwhelming delight, his salvation.

Now imagine the look on his face if the pastor were to shake his hand and say, "Now, my dear brother, read your Bible every day. It will tell you how to live. But I must warn you: You will find many promises in your Bible that you should not take to heart. You have just received the only promise God guarantees to fulfill. The others you will read about are 'iffy' at best. Our experience has shown that they are somewhat unreliable. But remember to pray every day. That will help you develop a relationship with the Lord. Worship him and give him thanks, and bring your requests just as he has said, but don't expect too many answers to your prayer requests. Be thankful for just a few."

I would be willing to bet the farm no pastor has ever said that.

However, I would also be willing to bet that the message has been heard in many other ways. Sadly, even in our testimonies. It has been heard in the testimonies that said,

"God didn't do what he said he would do, but he at least gave me peace about it. Or if I don't have peace, I'm willing to trust he knows best."

The sad and undeniably inconvenient truth is that even though we sometimes don't experience the manifestation of the promises, we can't honestly say the reason for it is that God chose not to fulfill his word. There are just too many places in scripture that tell us God always upholds his word. Therefore, there must be other reasons why these promises have not been manifested, or fulfilled, in our lives.

I know that makes us uncomfortable. We imagine something akin to witch hunts in the church to find out why prayers aren't answered, why accidents happen, or why physical abuse or a myriad of other curses occur. Horrible images emerge of the emotional torture such condemning activity might bring to already devastated victims. Those pictures make us want to back off from even looking at the problem. As one pastor said, "I'd prefer to think God was in control of everything, and just trust him."

That sounds wise and perhaps even comforting. In truth, I can easily identify with that pastor's desire because, as painful as it may be, sometimes accepting whatever happens as being from the hand of God is far less painful than some other options, such as accepting the fact that we just don't know enough about what happened, or perhaps even accepting some responsibility for our outcomes.

But what if, as painful as it may be to think so, it's simply not true that God planned those disasters, diseases, deaths and disappointments, even for some good reason, even if he has—as has happened in some cases—taken the evil and brought something good out if it?

What if God is looking at the horrible state our world is in and is grieving as much as we are? Grieving because Jesus paid a heavy price so his children could walk in life and light, not death and darkness, and yet they are still suffering insipid death, the effects of a curse brought into the earth millennia ago through man's original sin? A curse Jesus already bore in our stead.

Don't we, at least, have the responsibility to ourselves, to our children—my goodness, to God!—to find out if that's the case? Shouldn't we find out if God really is behind the mess?

If God really is responsible for our trouble, as some believe, and is righteous and just in all his ways, as the scriptures say, then we have to accept that all the bad stuff is really good in some way we can't imagine. But if he isn't behind it, then maybe we shouldn't retreat into an easy—but then, perhaps, not so easy after all—life of complacent non-engagement.

I must include a caution here. We are told not to judge someone else's walk with God. We are simply not qualified to do so. We are to judge our own walk and work out our own salvation with fear and trembling. We do that by searching the scriptures to find the truth and then examining our own lives in the light of what we find.

Surely, we can search to find out what his ways are, walk in them if we aren't already, and in doing so, as Paul said, become partakers of the inheritance of the saints—the inheritance Jesus already bought for us. An inheritance we are to enjoy not only in Heaven but also here on earth, in the very presence of our enemies.

THINKING ABOUT CHAPTER ELEVEN

SELF DISCOVERY QUESTIONS:

1. Have you ever looked around and lost hope in God because of what you saw?

2. Where do the scriptures say our hope is to come from?

3. Where do you find your hope?

4. Have you ever felt you have no part to play in your destiny?

KEEPERS' PRAYER:

Lord,

Help me never to be afraid of truth. You said it is truth that sets me free, so I want to know the whole truth and nothing but the truth, even if it's difficult to hear. I am willing to "buy the truth and sell it not" (Proverbs 23:23), but I'm depending on your Holy Spirit to teach me.

CHAPTER TWELVE

~

The Inheritance

"Thy testimonies have I taken as a heritage forever:
for they are the rejoicing of my heart."

~Psalm 119:111

~12~

DOESN'T THAT WORD "INHERITANCE" ring a bell? Isn't that what the testimony was originally all about—letting the children of Israel know about their inheritance?

Their inheritance was the blessing, and the blessing was offered in the covenant, and the covenant was expressed in laws and promises. Even though Psalm 78 doesn't use the words "inheritance" or "promises," the fact that it presents a reason for hope indicates promises are being passed down. Let's look at it again:

> *"We will not hide them from our children, shewing to the generation to come the praises of the Lord, and his strength, and his wonderful works that he hath done. For he established a testimony in Jacob, and appointed a law in Israel, which he commanded our fathers, that they should make them known to their children: That the generation to come might know them, even the children which should be born; who should arise and declare them to their children: That they might set their hope in God, and not forget the works of God and keep his commandments" (Psalm 78:4-7).*

If we are going to become keepers of the testimony, sharing it effectively with our children and others, we will have to come to terms with the fact that the testimony is not just about safely putting into their hands the precious treasure of the knowledge of salvation. It is also about sharing the knowledge of the inheritance available to us here on earth through the shed blood of Jesus. To do one without the other is to do a disservice to the testimony of Jesus.

We become more effective keepers of the testimony when we recognize that our inheritance is expressed in promises and that the manifestation of the promise is neither automatic nor at God's whim.

According to the Apostle Peter, these exceeding great and precious promises are the vehicle by which we are partakers of the divine nature (2 Peter 1:4). According to the writer of Hebrews, it is by faith and patience that we inherit the promises (Hebrews 6:12).

It would seem, then, that what the Divine Nature, God himself, wills for us is expressed in his promises but its manifestation is achieved by our participation, in faith and patience.

All of that must somehow be expressed in the testimony.

The children of Abraham were to tell their own children the ways and works of God—that is, the terms and effects of the covenant—so they would hope in him and walk in his ways. The result would be the covenant promises manifested to them, or in other words, fulfilled in their generation.

It seems that every testimony should have within it three components: firstly, a clear picture of the loving heart of God that expresses itself in a good and perfect plan for his children, which plan is, itself, partly expressed in his exceeding great and precious promises; secondly, a clear picture of how that plan is established in the life of a believer; and thirdly, clear proof of God's faithfulness to his word.

So here, then, is the anatomy of a testimony:

1. God's word: His promise: Our inheritance

2. God's ways: His written wisdom for us to walk out.

3. Evidence of God's character: Proof of his faithfulness.

The true testimony, therefore, shows the promise: God's word. It also shows the process: walking in his ways. And, finally, it shows the proof: visible evidence of God's faithfulness to keep his covenant.

Sometimes we've heard the promise. For example, we've heard about God's promise to provide for our needs.

Sometimes we've even been shown the proof. For instance, we have heard wonderful stories of missionaries and gospel pioneers who were desperately in need of food when, at the last moment, someone showed up at their door with bags of groceries.

More often than not, however, we have to listen very carefully in order to hear the process that the believer went through—the part they played in the story. Sometimes it is implicit in the story and easily identified upon reflection, like when the table has been set in preparation even though no food is in the pantry. Sometimes it may not seem to be there in a specific event, especially in events that have very little time between the problem and the proof, such as deliverance from destruction in the midst of an accident. But it is there, even if it is in someone else's intercession or in a lifestyle of trusting God as our strength.

Most of us prefer not to mention any part we play in our stories, perhaps because, as I mentioned earlier, we've heard those testimonies that focused mainly on the testifier. We probably don't want to appear to deliberately attract attention to ourselves, or even actually *get* credit we don't deserve, but telling the process isn't the sort of thing that attracts attention to oneself. Not when we understand why it is necessary.

It might help us be more transparent if we remember that we wouldn't even know what part is ours to play if God didn't tell us, nor would we be able to play it if he didn't help us. As my mother always says, "No glory be to me!" The glory is, and always will be, his.

The truth is we need to tell the process explicitly whenever we can because the hearers need to hear it. They need to hear it because, as we've seen by simply observing life, the promises are not always fulfilled just because we want them to be. We need to tell it because when the promises aren't manifested, or fulfilled, it is God's name—God's reputation—not ours, that suffers. For God's sake, and for our children's sake, let's tell them the process.

THINKING ABOUT CHAPTER TWELVE

SELF DISCOVERY QUESTIONS:

1. Have you ever thought much about your inheritance in Christ?

2. Did you ever think your inheritance was Heaven only?

3. Have you ever thought you would walk in your inheritance automatically, with no effort on your part?

KEEPERS' PRAYER:

Father,

I want my life to show your goodness and faithfulness. I confess I'd prefer not to have any part to play in receiving my inheritance, but I'm willing to learn to walk in your ways. You have said you will be my guide and counselor, so I trust you to counsel me wisely. I trust you to show me the process.

CHAPTER THIRTEEN

~

The Process

"The righteousness of thy testimonies is everlasting:
give me understanding and I shall live."

~Psalm 119:144

~13~

IT MAY BE HELPFUL TO TAKE A LOOK back at the testimonies of some of the early partners of covenant and find evidence of the process in their testimonies. I write their stories in *What's in a Name*. They are worth repeating here and I do so to use them as models. I apologize to those of you who have already read them but I saw no good purpose in trying to write them differently here.

(For those of you who have not yet read *What's in a Name*, I hope these stories spark an interest in the book—a book which will give wonderful insights into the name of the Lord and his exalted word.)

First there was Abraham. I quote from the tale already told:

> One of Abraham's stories is told in Genesis 22. God had given Abraham a son and had told him, "In Isaac shall thy seed be called." In other words, the promise God had given Abraham—that he would be a father of many nations—would be fulfilled through Isaac. Surprisingly, we later hear God telling Abraham to sacrifice Isaac as a burnt offering in the land of Moriah. Isaac, the son of promise, was to be killed on an altar.

Tradition suggests this command to sacrifice Isaac was a test of Abraham's love, obedience, or commitment to the Lord and, of course, he passed.

All right, then, let's watch closely. Just how did Abraham respond to God's command? How did he pass what must have been a profoundly painful test? Where did he find the strength to obey?

Hebrews 11: 17-19 tells us about what was going on in Abraham's mind and heart:

> *"By faith Abraham, when he was tried, offered up Isaac: and he that received the promises offered up his only begotten son, Of whom it was said, That in Isaac shall thy seed be called: accounting that God was able to raise him up, even from the dead; from whence he received him in a figure."*

It would seem Abraham expected God to bring Isaac back from the dead! Abraham's own words to his servants also indicate as much. Before he left them, Abraham said, "I and the lad will go yonder and worship, and come to you again." Unless he was lying to his servants, Abraham expected Isaac to return with him.

We know the rest of the story. As Abraham raised the knife to sacrifice his only son, the angel of the Lord spoke. Very welcome words reached his ears—"Abraham, lay not thine hand upon the lad,"—and Abraham looked up to see, behind him, a ram caught in a bush. This was the lamb Abraham had previously told Isaac about when he said to his questioning teenager, "The Lord will provide himself a lamb."

That's quite a testimony! We love to hear it and I imagine Isaac loved to tell it to his own children in the years that followed.

Did you notice something? It started with a promise. Abraham received a promise from God in which his son, Isaac, was to play an integral part. God was going to make Abraham the father of many nations and establish an everlasting covenant with Isaac and with his seed after him (Genesis 17:19). After the promise, lo and behold, a circumstance appeared which belied the promise. For Abraham, the contradictory circumstance came in the form of a command: Sacrifice Isaac on an altar. This instruction made it look as if God had changed his mind about Isaac and Isaac's seed.

Now we watch the process in this testimony.

The first thing we see is that Abraham obeyed. He prepared to sacrifice Isaac on an altar. But that's not all he did. He also held fast to the original promise he had been given. He acted in obedience to God but he did so still believing *in Isaac shall his seed be called.*

The result of this whole scenario—holding to the promise, giving glory to God as he did so, while obeying an instruction which certainly must have seemed contrary to the promise—was that Abraham experienced God to be Jehovah Jireh, his provider. The end of the matter showed the proof of God's faithfulness to his promise since it was, indeed, in Isaac that Abraham's seed was called.

Abraham has been called the father of our faith and, no doubt, holds that title because of the very act of faith we've talked about here—an act that furthered God's plan to bring his own son, our Savior, into the world.

It would appear, then, that *the process which stood between the promise given to Abraham and its fulfillment was called faith*—that is, holding fast to the promise in the face of contrary circumstances, and acting in obedience to whatever God commanded.

Another Bible story—that of David and Goliath—again shows the way the process works. And again, I'll pick it up as it's told in *What's in a Name.*

The first book of Samuel, chapter 17 records what is probably the most famous of David's stories. It happened when David was still a young man, long before anyone sang songs of his bravery and skill in battle. His father had sent him to take food to his brothers who were at the battle site where the Philistines and their trump card, the formidable warrior-giant, Goliath, held King Saul and the men of Israel at a standstill.

As a shepherd, young David had spent much time on the hillsides caring for his father's sheep. No doubt, during long days and nights when the quiet was interrupted only by the bleating of the sheep and the occasional pesky predator, he meditated on the God of his fathers. We can confidently assume David spent considerable time thinking about God on those hills, not only because we know the many worship songs he wrote during those days but also because we can see his fathers' God immediately came to mind when he saw what was going on in the valley of Elah that day.

Listen to this youngster:

Vs 26: "Who is this uncircumcised Philistine, that he should defy the armies of the living God?"

This question gives us our first clue that David knows something God has said. He has heard a promise that has prophesied something to him. Listen to what he does with it.

The story continues:

Hear the outrage in his voice! David saw the men of Israel cowering in the presence of trouble and knew there was something very wrong with this scene. Here was the problem: this man, Goliath, was uncircumcised. He, therefore, had no covenant with God. God had made him no promises. Yet, here in this valley, the children of Israel, who were the possessors of the promises, were the fearful ones.

It was unthinkable; David knew it just shouldn't be. He began to speak out—quite annoyingly, I imagine—to everyone around him, "God will deliver us from this scourge!"

His older brother scolded him for his insolence and presumption, to which spunky young David replied, "What have I done? Is there not a cause?" David was saying, "Don't I have reason to say these things, considering our covenant?"

Notice, here, that David is not dissuaded by his brother or by the apparent cowardice of the soldiers in Saul's army. He refuses to let go of the promise. We begin to see the process.

The fiery young shepherd preached his message to all who would listen to him, and finally the soldiers took him to King Saul himself. With vivid accounts of his past victories by God's hand—such as the stories about the lions and bears that tried and failed to steal his sheep— David attempted to persuade Saul to let him face the bone-chilling Goliath. Miracle of miracles, it worked!

I've often wondered what Saul saw in David's eyes or heard in his voice that made him decide to send him out—a boy against a giant, a singing shepherd against a proven warrior. Whatever it was, I'll bet Goliath, too, saw it in David's fearless run toward him on the field of battle and heard it in his shouted declaration: Vs 45: "You came to me with a sword, and with a spear, and with a shield: but I come to you in the name of the Lord of hosts, the God of the armies of Israel, whom thou hast defied."

Why such bravado? Could it simply be that just like Abraham, who had the word of the Lord that assured him Isaac would be the one from whom his progeny would spring, David had a promise he expected to be fulfilled?

David certainly would have known deliverance from their enemies was one of God's promises to his people. Deuteronomy 28:7 says, "The Lord shall cause thine enemies that rise up against thee to be smitten before thy face: they shall come out against thee one way, and flee before thee seven ways."

Israel's covenant promised them smitten enemies. David knew that. Could that be why he knew he would smite Goliath that day? Listen to what he confidently yelled to the threatening Goliath in verse 46: "This day will the Lord deliver thee into mine hand; and I will smite thee."

In this one amazing statement I hear young David's confidence God would uphold the words recorded in Deuteronomy 28: "thine enemies…smitten before thy face."

This same verse told him his enemies would flee before him seven ways.

Well, did David's enemies flee? Indeed they did. Verse 51 tells us, "and when the Philistines saw their champion was dead, they fled." Imagine that!

There it is again: first, the promise; then, the process— David's holding fast to the promise even in the face of contrary circumstances and, by his words and actions, giving glory to God. In this case, when David saw the state of affairs of the Israelite army, he could have been tempted to say, "I wonder why God has not kept his promise. Here's a vicious enemy who isn't fleeing. Maybe God has some reason not to keep his promise in this case." But notice that David didn't say any such thing. He held to the promise in the face of its apparent denial.

I think the words contained in the promise "flee *before thee*" told David that he, or someone, had to get involved in the process. And so he did. David's action, born of faith in the promise and energized by the hope the promise held, was getting involved in the fight.

And finally we see the proof of God's faithfulness. What a testimony David finally was able to give his children! What praise to God, and hope in God, was the result!

Another story referred to in *What's in a Name* is one most of us know from Sunday school—that of three famous Hebrew children.

Here we go again:

> The story of Shadrach, Meshach, and Abednego is told in chapter three of the book of Daniel.

Daniel 3:14-18

14, Nebuchadnezzar spoke and said unto them, Is it true, O Shadrach, Meshach, and Abednego, do not ye serve my gods, nor worship the golden image which I have set up?

15, Now if ye be ready that at what time ye hear the sound of the cornet, flute, harp, sackbut, psaltry, and dulcimer, and all kinds of music, ye fall down and worship the image I have made, well: but if ye worship not, ye shall be cast the same hour into the midst of a fiery furnace; and who is that God that shall deliver you out of my hands?

16, Shadrach, Meshach, and Abednego, answered and said to the king, O Nebuchadnezzar, we are not careful to answer thee in this matter.

17, If it be so, our God whom we serve is able to deliver us from the burning fiery furnace, and he will deliver us out of thine hand, O king.

18, But if not, be it known unto thee, O king, that we will not serve thy gods, nor worship the golden image which thou hast set up.

We know and love the rest of the story. They were thrown into the flames but, suddenly, miraculously, they were joined by a big fellow who looked so powerful he appeared to be like the son of God, and, wonder of wonders, the four of them walked freely in the fire.

When the king saw this, he had an immediate conversion experience. Not surprising, since when one who looks like the son of God shows up in a conflict, you definitely want to be found on his side. Whatever Nebuchadnezzar's motivation, whether change of heart or survival instinct, he altered his furnace policy. Listen to him as he tells our sweet-smelling, no-smoke-on-'em young heroes to come hither out of the fire. God delivered his children even when it looked as if all hope was lost.

This familiar story often has been taught to encourage complete dedication and obedience to God in the face of adversity. However, sometimes we have been led, incorrectly, to believe those three brave boys went into the flames thinking maybe God would not help them. A common misconception, this idea comes from the words the boys, themselves, used in verse 18 when talking to the king, "Our God will deliver us…but if not, we will not serve your gods."

Watch closely here and you'll see the promise stated. It may not be explicit but it is definitely there.

In fact, that is not what this passage is saying. Others may have thought hope was lost but not these young Hebrews. If we listen to them very carefully we realize these boys were convinced God would deliver them. See here what the boys were really thinking and saying:

> *Vs 17, "If it be so, our god whom we serve is able to deliver us from the fiery furnace, and he will deliver us out of thine hand O king."*

If what be so? If the king's threat be so! These boys were actually saying they doubted the king's ability to carry out his threat. Here's the king's threat:

> *Vs 15, "If ye worship not, ye shall be cast that same hour into the midst of a burning fiery furnace."*

Wait for it! Here comes their statement of the promise they were holding to:

So in verse 17 the boys are telling the king that if he throws them in, "our God **can** and **will** deliver us out of your hand." According to this, they didn't doubt either God's ability or His willingness to deliver them.

Let's look at verses 17 and 18 together:

> *"If it be so (that is, if you throw us in the furnace) our God can and will deliver us from your hand. But if not (that is, if you do not throw us in the furnace), we still will not bow down and worship the image."*

In other words: "No negotiation! No deal! No way!"

Why would these three Hebrews say "Our God will deliver us" as well as "Our God can deliver us"? We remember, of course, they had heard the stories of the great deliverances of the past and had seen the hand of God deliver their people more than once. History told them God could deliver but what made them say he will?

Even though the specific promises weren't stated in this story exactly as written in scripture, we can, in hindsight, recognize in their statements to the king their confidence in what their covenant provided.

As the excerpt from *What's in a Name* goes on, we see the covenant promises with which these boys would have been familiar.

> (…what made them say He will?) It probably was because they knew the scriptures. We can safely assume they did so because we saw evidence of that fact in their diligent and meticulous efforts to obey the law. Remember, these were the boys who earlier refused to eat the king's food because their covenant told them it was unlawful to do so. Surely, because of their knowledge of their covenant, they also would have known that in Isaiah 43:2 it was recorded that God had said, "When thou passest through the waters I will be with thee: when thou walkest through the fire, thou shalt not be burned; neither shall the flame kindle upon thee."
>
> They probably recalled verses from Psalms that told of God's willingness to deliver all who fear him. Psalm 34:7, for example, says, "The angel of the Lord encampeth round about them that fear him and delivereth them." The only proviso of this promise was a reverential fear of God and it is apparent from their actions that these young fellows feared God. That's how they got into this trouble in the first place: obedience to God's directive to worship no other gods, an obedience no doubt born out of a proper fear and respect for God.
>
> They knew the commandments; they knew the promises.

Can you see how this testimony unfolded? First there was the promise or, perhaps more accurately, promises. Then we see the process: In the face of contrary circumstances—in this case they were actually thrown in the flames—they acted in obedience to their part of the covenant and still held fast to the promises, giving glory to God by their words and actions.

Actually, there were two acts of obedience going on here. First there was their refusal to bow in worship to someone who wasn't God and, also, their holding fast to the promise as they did so, giving God glory declaring, "Our God will deliver us!" Both of these were part of God's directions to his people: Believe and obey.

What a marvelous testimony to the faithfulness of God resulted from that event! What hope for those who would face such a circumstance themselves! In fact, how many of us think of those three boys when we're going through our own furnace of affliction, and say with them, "When I walk through the fire, I will not be burned!"

In all of these accounts, the process was clear and simple. It still is today.

Whenever I need clarification or simplification in dealing with a problem or challenge to my faith, I think of one of my favorite childhood Sunday school choruses—a chorus which succinctly presents the process. It went like this:

> *"Trust and obey, for there's no other way*
> *To be happy in Jesus but to trust and obey."*

THINKING ABOUT CHAPTER THIRTEEN

SELF DISCOVERY QUESTIONS:

1. Have you ever recognized the process in the God stories you have heard, either from the Bible or from the lives of your family and friends?

2. What contrary circumstance has told you that God is not keeping a promise he's made to you?

3. Are you willing to hold to his promise in spite of what you see?

KEEPERS' PRAYER:

Dear Father,

Help me to always hear you clearly, believe you completely, and obey you quickly. Help me to trust and obey.

CHAPTER FOURTEEN

~

In Our Hands

*"My soul hath kept thy testimonies;
and I love them exceedingly."*

~Psalm119:167

~14~

WHETHER OR NOT WE TELL our stories is our own decision. Many of us may believe that our walk with God is private and therefore might feel uncomfortable sharing our experiences. I hope this book gives you pause for thought about your choices in that regard.

I started this book with the story of an event that changed my thinking about the power of the testimony. Before I finish, I want to share more stories that bless me every time I recall them. Even though some of them are very simple and might seem insignificant to all but me, the bottom line is that they show God's faithfulness. For that reason, I happily include them. We'll look for parts of the anatomy of a testimony as we go.

Even though I love this first story, I am somewhat hesitant to tell it right after talking about our heroes of the faith because it in no way is like their stories.

Actually, that's not quite true. They are alike in one way. This story, like theirs, required an action born of faith.

The story took place several years ago, at the very beginning of my *conscious* faith walk, just when I was learning to rely, on purpose, on what God had said about his relationship with me as a believer. Although this story and the process involved in it may both seem simple and small, it felt pretty big to me at the time. Even now, there are times I go back to it for encouragement.

I had been a believer for a long time but had, during the early years, pretty much gone about my days and done life without a conscious awareness of God's involvement in it, except on Sundays, of course, and maybe Wednesdays, cell group night. But now things were different. Now I was on a deliberate quest to learn.

Specifically, in this story, I was learning to see God as my provider, based on the promise, "My God shall supply all your need according to his riches in glory by Christ Jesus." I was also learning how to walk out many instructions in God's word such as giving financially to different ministries whose work I believed in.

On that particular month, however, my budgeted supply fell short of my actual demand. I had a rather large unexpected expense—I think it may have been a car repair bill. As I wrote cheques at the beginning of that month I was tempted to refrain from giving to one ministry we had committed to support. I thought I should hold on to the money in order to pay that bill I hadn't planned on. The amount wasn't enough to cover the bill but it would have helped.

I remember standing at my ironing board talking to God about it. To be honest, I was complaining. I whined, "You know, I probably need the money more than they [the ministry organization] do."

In fact, the more I thought about it, the more I began to get angry with those people who wanted my support when they were no doubt better off than I.

I had worked up quite a head of steam in that direction when I heard in my heart, *"Satan comes immediately to steal the word."*

I was taken aback—shocked to realize where this irritation had come from. Not from reason. Not from common sense or from righteous indignation. It came from a thief.

Too stubborn to let my fledgling faith walk be crippled by disobedience born of fear of lack, I immediately left my ironing board, went to my desk, and wrote the cheque. Then, before I could change my mind, I rushed down the street and popped it into the mailbox.

Back at my ironing board, I was feeling pretty proud of myself for overcoming fear. Then, thinking more about that bill, I thought, "You should call the school board and ask if they owe you any money."

A substitute teacher at the time, I kept very close tabs on where and when I taught and when I was paid for each session. I was pretty sure no one owed me anything. Still, I went to my record book just to be certain. Sure enough, just as I thought, my pay was up to date. I went back to ironing.

Minutes later, I had that strange prompting again, "Call the school board and ask if they owe you money."

How I struggled with that! How foolish I would feel making the call and asking that question! I had no reason to ask. None, that is, except a strong inner impression. After a long while I thought, *Oh well, they don't know me anyway. I'll do it. After all, I don't have to look anyone in the eye with a phone call.* So I called.

"Which dates have you not received pay for?" the school board staffer asked.

"None that I know of, but could you check to see if you owe me anything?"

I could tell she was puzzled. "Alright, I'll check your file." As she was returning from her search of my teaching and pay records I could hear her muttering, "Now that's odd."

Back on the phone, she said, "I don't know why this hasn't been sent already, but there's a cheque here for retroactive pay. Substitutes were given a raise some months back, so you should have received this long ago." The raise had been considerable and the cheque was much more than enough to pay that unexpected and troublesome bill.

To this day, I believe that the initial act of faith (keeping our commitment to the ministry), made in response to God's promise to meet my needs, opened my ears to hear the words which led me to his provision, "Go call the school board." I have always been thankful I listened to the Lord that day and fulfilled that commitment—a commitment which, as I mentioned earlier, wasn't even close to the amount in that cheque. Not just thankful for a paid bill, I was then and still am thankful for the lesson in hearing, believing, and obeying. It paid great dividends in the years to come.

Let's look at the anatomy of that testimony.

First there was the promise: God will meet all your needs.

Then the instruction came: "Keep your commitment."

I didn't know it then, but by deciding to trust God's faithfulness and thereby hold fast to his promise and obey the first instruction, I was beginning a necessary process. In fact, I'm sure that without that first small obedience in sending off that check I may not have heard the second instruction: "Call the school board." That call to the school board office gave me undeniable proof of the faithfulness of God, who had already said he was my provider.

Since then we have lived many stories in which God showed himself to be a very faithful provider. In every one of them, several of which I mention in *What's in a Name,* there was a period of time where we had nothing to go on but God's word and, in later years, our experience of his faithfulness.

Another occasion that comes to mind was when our daughter, Gillian, was preparing to go to university. After some research and prayer, she decided on Oral Roberts University in Tulsa, Oklahoma. We checked it out, as well as several other schools, and agreed ORU would be a good place for her to do her undergraduate degree. However, although we had—we thought—enough money set aside for her education, we had always thought she would study at the university in our hometown. Unfortunately, our savings would cover only one semester at ORU, especially since the Canadian dollar was faring rather poorly in comparison to the American dollar in those days.

I was secretly hoping that either Gillian or her father would see this was not the right plan but I eventually realized we had to move forward. However, we did tell Gillian we would not go into debt for this project so God would have to provide the extra funds needed, or one semester would be the extent of her ORU experience.

After Gillian went off to Tulsa that first semester I received a call from a woman I had spoken with briefly at a university function a few nights previously. We had chatted that evening about my experiences teaching in a private school in Texas and now she asked would I be willing to visit with the principal of the private school where her children were students. The school needed someone to fill in for a teacher who was about to take sick leave. To shorten a long story, the position became mine and, with it, Gillian's tuition for the second semester.

Of course, if it had been left up to me, we would have seen all the money we needed for Gillian's education in one nice big lump sum but, not surprisingly, that was not to be. Instead, more often then not, even a month before the beginning of each semester we still didn't have the money. However, as each new semester approached we met it with more and more confidence in God's faithfulness because by the time each semester arrived we had the money needed. The amazing thing about it was that, every time, it came from a source outside our normal financial pipeline.

In this testimony, the promises we based our requests on—and held to constantly—were the ones that told us God would direct our steps (Psalm 37:23), and he was able to give us everything we needed to be successful in every good work (2 Corinthians 9:8).

The act of faith in this instance was sending Gillian to ORU, using up all the money we had set aside for her education while refusing to let go of the promises. The proof, of course, we've seen.

But enough about money! We have also seen God's faithfulness in many other areas of life. This next story has nothing to do with finances. It is one of my favorite testimonies and one which had huge significance in my life and the lives of several of my friends.

The story is from the time years ago when one of the cell groups from our church met at our house. In our group there was a woman who had been on dialysis for several years. In almost every meeting she asked us to pray with her that she would receive a new kidney. In my zeal, I wanted to ask for a new one without surgery—after all, God is able—but she wasn't ready to join me in that audacious request so, instead, our group prayed that she would remain healthy until one became available through the normal course of events.

The day soon came when she called to say she was on her way to the airport to fly to another province to get her new kidney. I prayed with her that all would go well and that she would come home with a good working kidney.

At our next cell group meeting our pastor gave us the bad news. The surgery had gone well, but her body rejected the new kidney. She would be coming home and returning to life with dialysis.

We were deflated and discouraged. We could imagine how devastated she must be, and every one of us hurt for her. Before the meeting was over that night we prayed for her once more—this time that God would comfort her heart and give her safe travel home.

As we prayed, it slowly began to dawn on us that this bad report did not present a good reason to back off from our original prayer. We remembered that we could well be the only people praying for her since her family members weren't believers, as far as we knew, and might not even know to pray. No matter what, we shouldn't give up so readily. We were just now learning to hold on to the word of God when we prayed and, after all, didn't the Lord say those that ask receive?

After some discussion, we all agreed to hold fast to that word. We would keep looking for God's hand at work on behalf of our friend.

At church the following Sunday, I sat at the piano with tears dripping off my chin as our pastor told what transpired in our friend's God story in the days following our meeting— a story he'd had confirmed by her doctors at the hospital.

Apparently, the hospital staff had hooked her up to a dialysis machine one more time before sending her to the airport. In her words, she "felt a bang in my chest" and then found she was leaving her body. Feeling better than she'd felt in some time, she found herself going upward toward a light.

She didn't know how long this journey lasted but soon she woke up, back in her body, with several doctors standing around her putting away medical resuscitation instruments. She heard one say, "You'll need to notify the family." When she spoke to them, asking, "What happened?" they turned and stared in shock. Then, wonder of wonders, the new kidney began to work.

The doctors kept her there for three more days, putting her through more tests in order to find out what had happened. Then, failing to find a medical reason for any of it, they sent her home with a working kidney.

Our friend lived for many more years and was blessed to see her family come to faith in Jesus.

I know someone may be thinking, "Well, God had a plan for her, and he would have made things work out for her even if your group hadn't persisted in prayer."

That certainly may be true, but to think that way will bring death to a prayer life. We must always connect the answers we receive to the prayers we prayed. That's not prideful; it's merely respectful of God's assessment of the situation. James 5:16 tells us the prayer of the righteous avails much. That means our prayers are supposed to make a difference and, simply because it says so, we should expect them to do so.

So here, again, we see the anatomy of a God story.

First, the promise: He that asks receives.

Then, the contrary circumstance: The rejected kidney.

Next, the process: The act of obedience—being patient, and refusing to back down or give up what we knew Jesus bought for us at great cost. Hearing and obeying God's directions is crucial in any conflict.

And, finally, what wonderful proof of God's faithfulness! Trusting in God's faithfulness seems to be one of the key ingredients in the making of a testimony. In fact, one way we give glory to him in the midst of our circumstance is refusing to agree with anything other than what God has already said about it.

There was a time years ago—seems like ages ago, now— when I wasn't convinced of God's faithfulness to do what he said he'd do. I should have been so convinced because I had grown up in church and I knew God was good. I knew he was merciful. I knew he loved us enough to make sure we had a way to escape eternal damnation. In fact, I knew a lot about God.

I had even learned to pray in most situations and ask that God's will be done but, in most cases, if not in all, I had little idea of what his will might be. Truth be told, I had stopped praying even that prayer, although for a long time I didn't quite realize I had.

Life pointed out my prayerlessness one day when our daughter was just a little girl, not much past toddlerhood. My husband was an officer in the Canadian navy at that time, and away on deployment, and my friend Pam was babysitting Gillian for the evening while I joined other officers' wives for the traditional wives' night out. When I got home that evening, Pam informed me, sort of with tongue in cheek but with a slight ring of sincerity, "You aren't raising that child right!"

"What do you mean?" I shot back, somewhat offended because I considered myself a conscientious mother.

"That child knows nothing about prayer!" she accused. "Her tummy was hurting, so I asked if I could pray for her tummy to get better and she said, 'No. My mother will give me some medicine when she gets home.'"

I laughed. Kids say the darnedest things.

But, alas, it was true. The child knew nothing about prayer.

Here I stood—a church-going, choir-singing, Bible-reading Christian who was reluctant to pray out loud for my little girl *in front of her*. I loved my daughter dearly, and I did pray for her every time she was sick, but silently, because I didn't want her disappointed, as I always was, if God didn't answer my prayer with any positive action on our behalf.

Truthfully and sadly, even my silent prayer was prayed with a bit of an attitude because I really didn't expect him to answer and thought it was really too bad of him because, after all, what had she ever done to deserve his lack of care?

Thankfully, in the years following, I learned that prayer wasn't just asking God to do me some favor and hoping he would see things my way. It was much more than that. I learned something about the part the promise plays in any prayer.

I learned that praying prayers based on God's promises puts us in the position of praying according to his will. Such prayers are part of God's ways and of the working out of the covenant.

As Gillian grew up she learned those things as well, simply from being involved in the process as our family eventually began to practice living by faith in God's written word even in the midst of circumstances that were obviously contrary to that word.

Many years later, when we were living in Texas, Gillian, a young teenager by this time, asked if she could go home to Canada for a visit. It didn't look possible to me. My husband was in a doctoral program and I was teaching in a private Christian school. That translated into low funds, so I explained we couldn't afford it right then.

Always a persistent soul, she asked, "If we get some extra money, can I go then?"

I sighed. If we were to find extra money, I had several other places it needed to go and told her so.

But Gillian had been raised on the scripture in Matthew 18:19 which said, "If any two of you shall agree on earth as touching any thing that they shall ask, it shall be done for them of my Father in Heaven," so she persisted still, "Okay, I get that, but if I pray will you agree with my prayer?"

Sometimes we don't want to agree with a child's prayer, especially when money is involved, unless we are able to answer it ourselves, so at first I was reluctant. However, I quickly realized I needed to trust God with Gillian's prayer as well as her trip to Canada. This was training ground for her own walk of faith, which meant she needed to experience God's faithfulness in response to her own prayers.

So I committed myself to the prayer of agreement. I took a deep breath and said, "I will agree with your prayer for a trip home. But the money will have to come to you, personally. Agreed?"

"Agreed!"

In our family, as a rule, we don't discuss our financial needs with anyone but God, so I'm pretty sure no one knew about either Gillian's prayer or her wish to go home to see her friends. Some time later I got a phone call. During the conversation, an unexpected question arose, "What's Gillian doing this summer? Do you think she'd like to come home for a visit? I just got some extra money and I thought of her."

Shocked because this person didn't make a habit of such offers, I could hardly contain myself as I exulted, "Yes, I'm sure she'd love that."

"Good! I'll send her the money and she can get a ticket and come whenever she wants."

I'm sure you can imagine a teenager's response when she realized she'd be getting to hang out with her friends back in Canada—and with her parents half a continent away. Such whooping and dancing! Such praise to God!

There are many more stories of the goodness of God in my own life and the lives of my friends and family, but I'd like you to think about your own testimonies. I know if you've walked with the Lord for a while you have more than a few. You may have had disappointments as well but, for now, set them aside. (I'm not suggesting you ignore them; God can handle your questions.) For now focus on your testimonies of God's faithfulness. Maybe even do it just as an experiment. Feel the hope that rises up in you as you do. Let your own testimonies prophesy to you.

Your testimonies will do the same for others who hear them. They'll do that for your children.

In this twenty-first century—and, perhaps, especially in our Western culture—it may be difficult to find opportunities to share our stories with our family since children of all ages are kept inordinately busy with sports, special classes, and, of course, on line activities of different kinds. If we add to that the busyness of adult responsibilities we can see why parents sometimes feel that, instead of living *with* their children, they live *parallel* to them.

However, if you are watching for teachable moments you will find them. The moments are there somewhere—like when you drive your children to school, clean the garage together, shop at the mall and stop for a treat, or perhaps even when you sit around the Thanksgiving table, demolishing the carcass of the turkey or enjoying one more piece of pumpkin pie.

If your children are teenagers, or maybe even adults, they might not appear to enjoy those moments at first. In fact, if you make it too much of a production, you both may feel somewhat awkward about the endeavor. So keep it casual. It will help if you find a jumping off point from something they have said, so the moment doesn't appear calculated.

After a while, the moments will happen spontaneously and easily. Eventually, your children will enjoy these times with you, especially if you give them time to talk as well, and if you are just as interested in what they have to say as you are in what you want to say to them.

Whatever happens, don't give up. Your time is a gift no one but you can give your children, and although anyone can repeat your stories, they are best heard from your lips.

THINKING ABOUT CHAPTER FOURTEEN

SELF DISCOVERY QUESTIONS:

1. Can you identify the promise of God that started your own testimonies?

2. Can you see the process in your testimonies?

3. Can you recall stories that show the proof of God's faithfulness in your life?

4. Do you go back to your own testimonies to find encouragement in each new conflict?

KEEPERS' PRAYER:

Father,

Thank you for my stories. In every challenge I meet, help me to trust you and have faith in your promises.

CHAPTER FIFTEEN

~

For the Children

"And when thy son shalt say unto thee in time to come, saying, What mean the testimonies, and the statutes and the judgments, which the Lord our God hath commanded you? Then shalt thou say to thy son, We were Pharaoh's bondmen in Egypt; and the Lord brought us out of Egypt with a mighty hand: And the Lord showed signs and wonders, great and small, before our eyes: And He brought us out from thence, that He might bring us in, to give us a land which he sware unto our fathers."

~Deuteronomy 6:20-23

~15~

THIS BOOK HAS BEEN about the testimony, but it has been for the children. Over and over in the Bible we see how important God considers our relationship with them to be. Hopefully, this book has shown how important our walk with God is to our children.

Our children need our example. It is our gift to them just as Abraham's example, as part of the commanding and the training, was his gift to Isaac.

We will never be called upon to offer our children in the way Abraham was and we will never battle a physical giant as David did, or face a literal fiery furnace as did the three Hebrews, but there can be no doubt we will be called upon to act in faith, just as they did, in many circumstances of life. When that happens, we will have to follow the same process they followed in order to attain the same victories.

One weapon that will empower us during challenging times will be recalling the testimonies we've lived and heard. Hopefully, our own stories and those of our family and friends will have shown the process which must be part of our new testimony-in-the-making.

As a teacher, I am at this point compelled by years of habit to review why each part of the testimony is necessary.

First, the promise must be included in our testimonies because even as God's existence doesn't prophesy specifics, neither does his action for one person necessarily provide prophecy and hope for someone else. Not even the wonderful attributes of God's character, such as his love, goodness, and faithfulness, will give us hope unless we also have his promises. A testimony which doesn't include, either explicitly or implicitly, the promise God kept, actually leaves out the prophecy!

What gives hope is the fact that God has actually said something specific in regard to our situation—that is, he has made a promise—and that he is faithful to do what he says. The prophecy is in the promise; the faithfulness is seen in its fulfillment.

For example, in the first story in this book—my Texan Terror story—the promise my husband and I held to, for the most part at least, in our morning prayers for the boys was the one found in 2 Peter 1:3, which says, "According as his divine power hath given unto us all things that pertain unto life and godliness, through the knowledge of him that hath called us to glory and virtue." That verse told me—prophesied to me—that God would provide whatever wisdom, knowledge, or help I needed that pertained to this life situation.

And, as the story shows, he did just that.

And, again, why should part of our story be the process we went through?

The answer is simple: It's because our children need to know the unabridged truth. Because of the death and defeat much too prevalent in this fallen world—all of which might make them think God is either not paying attention or simply doesn't do what he says—our children need to know the part they play in receiving God's promises fulfilled. Without the whole truth, our children are at risk in a dangerous world.

They need to be assured that salvation, *with all the provision and promise it entails*, is for whosoever will, not just for a special few who are especially blessed. Both of those words are important: "whosoever" and "will."

Because of all they see around them, our children need to know they can find in the Bible precious promises that God wants to bring to pass in their lives. They also need to know how to appropriate those promises.

They need to know it is okay to hold fast to those promises in the midst of circumstances that are downright contrary to what the Lord has promised. They need permission to hope in God and, in doing so, find the courage to never give up. Their will has to be involved.

Telling our children the small but vital part we had to play in our story—that we simply held on to what we knew of God's will and his faithfulness, and then obeyed any directions we were given—will give them the courage to do the same.

We spend a lot of time, money, and effort to make sure our children have what they need to make them happy, productive, and successful. We teach them God's laws, as directed in Psalm 78, so they will do right. We take them to good churches with good education departments and good youth groups so they'll have godly influences. We send them to good schools and the best colleges and universities we can afford so they'll have all the knowledge, skills, associations, and tools they need to fulfill their dreams and callings.

All of these things are great and, certainly, needful, but our children need more than these, as necessary as they are. They need the prophecy of their parents' testimony—stories of God's faithfulness in the lives of the people they know best.

That is what the testimonies were to my precious Texan Terrors. They were prophecy. For a time during those mornings in our stuffy portable classroom, the boys heard prophecy which gave them hope. Somehow, that hope softened their young hearts.

Before I finish this book, I have to include this thought: Just as in my Texan Terrors story I had to address my unloving attitude, so must each of us take a good look at our own heart because it is extremely important that our testimonies be shared from a place of love.

Don't misunderstand me. We don't need to have a perfect life's record in order to qualify to share our testimonies. After all, God didn't require perfection in order for us to receive the grace—the *undeserved* favor—from which the testimonies came. Still, we have to realize that if we haven't lived before our children a life characterized, for the most part, by love and integrity, their hearts *may* be closed to hearing *from us* the testimony of God's love and faithfulness.

If that is the case, we need not despair. After all, we aren't alone in this endeavor.

Remember how in my Terrors' story God turned our situation around and opened my students' hearts as well as mine? He will do the same for each of us if we ask him to and then follow his directions.

God is definitely on our side in this effort. Remember, he is the one who told us to keep the testimony—and with good reason. Just as we regularly face challenges, often from giants who try to take the land God has given us, our children will face them as well. God wants our children to overcome those enemies.

Our children will make mistakes. Like their parents, they will have struggles and will sometimes fail. Life is not perfect because none of us is perfect, but living our destiny doesn't depend on perfection. God loves to redeem our mistakes and rejoices with us when we use them to help us grow. The examples of our Bible heroes show us that.

Just think about David. We all know he wasn't perfect, but none of us will say he didn't fulfill his God-given destiny as king. Think of how glorious were the victories that he won through God, and how rich the heritage he left for us all.

Abraham wasn't perfect, but those of us who are Christ's are still called Abraham's seed (Galatians 3:29). The example of his faith has benefited many generations, and to this very day it teaches us!

Shall I speak of Moses, who didn't make it into the Promised Land; Peter, who swore that he didn't know Jesus; or Paul, whose misguided zeal drove him to execute many of the first Christians?

Obviously, even though mankind has had a consistently imperfect record, we know of many great destinies fulfilled. Psalm 37:24 tells us that though a good man falls he is not utterly cast down, for "the Lord upholds him with his hand." That last phrase is no doubt why those destinies were fulfilled. It was God who made the difference.

It is God who will make the difference for our children. Even though challenges are par for the course on this dark earth, defeat is not God's plan for our children. Many scriptures indicate that his plan is that they be overcomers.

What a glorious truth: In spite of their natural tendency to mess up occasionally, our children, like their parents, are called to be overcomers! John wrote about it in his first general letter to the relatively newborn church: "… this is the victory that overcomes the world, even our faith" (1 John 5:4).

That faith, as I mention in *What's in a Name*, is a power-filled gift from God which comes from believing his word and which we exercise as we hold fast to and act on that word.

In order to become the overcomers they were designed and destined to be, and in order to live the abundant life bought for them by precious blood, our children need to go into each battle armed with three God-ordained weapons: knowledge of God's promises, understanding of his ways, and confidence in his faithfulness. These three will enable them to do the believing and obeying necessary for their victory.

That *may* happen without our help; after all, we aren't the only influence in our children's lives. But we are the first influence, and probably by far the most invested influence— on this earth at least—and there can be no doubt we have a part to play in helping our children become all they were meant to be.

When our children hear from our own lips what it means to walk with God, when they see how we respond to his word, and when they recognize the proofs of his goodness and faithfulness even in our imperfect lives, they will find their most empowering inheritance.

In sharing our testimonies, we would do well to remember that patience is a key to victory in every worthy undertaking. Just as God's promises are the seed that bring the harvest of his will and purposes in our lives, so, also, our testimonies are seed for a future harvest in the lives of our children and others, and seeds take time to grow. If we remember that fact we won't become weary in well-doing.

See the precious harvest from that seed: In time, our children will, in the midst of whatever their generation brings, learn to declare the Lord's word and his faithfulness, prophesy their God-given future, and see its fulfillment by walking in his ways.

It may seem a small thing, to tell a story. It takes little time and, if the time chosen is right, little effort; even so, don't underestimate its value. For something so seemingly minor among the more obviously important activities in a day, it can have a huge effect on our children.

But first we have to live the stories. That takes both time and effort. When we perceive each conflict we encounter as a testimony in the making and courageously see it through to its rightful end—a witness to the loving kindness, truth, and righteous judgment of God—we play our part well.

If the testimony of Jesus really is the spirit of prophecy—and it is—then let's allow our testimony to become someone else's prophecy, to the glory of God. Let's live the stories and tell them to our children.

That has been his plan, all along.

THINKING ABOUT CHAPTER FIFTEEN

SELF DISCOVERY QUESTIONS:

1. Would you prefer to think that you and your children hold no responsibility for your outcomes in life?

2. Do you recognize that wherever there is authority, or free will, there is responsibility?

3. Does it help to know you need never be alone in any battle of life?

4. Are you willing, for God's sake and for the children's sake, to search for the truth?

KEEPERS' PRAYER:

Father God,
    This has been quite a journey, and it's not over yet. Thank You for your presence with me on this road. I am so glad I never have to travel alone, and I'm thankful for all you have provided—"all things that pertain unto life and godliness"—in my walk with you. May my life's stories show your faithfulness, and may my testimonies never fail to prophesy hope to all who hear them. May my children, in their turn, be keepers of the testimony.

ABOUT THE AUTHOR

Born and raised in Canada on the east coast of Newfoundland, Fay Rowe has also lived on the not-so-far-east coast in Halifax, Nova Scotia, and on the far west coast in Victoria, British Columbia. As well, she lived for several years in the United States while her husband attended university in College Station, Texas. Now Fay is glad to have settled at long last in London, Ontario, with her husband, Glenn, and their adopted barn cat, Casey.

As a teacher of fourth graders and junior high students, and in settings such as Sunday morning church services, Wednesday night Bible studies, women's groups and conference events, Fay has shared powerful insights with people of all ages. Her passion for teaching was translated into a passion for writing with the publication of her first book, *What's in a Name: Rediscovering the Integrity of God*, and now this, her latest book, **Keepers of the Testimony**. In each of her books, Fay communicates truths that have empowered a great many lives and which, she is convinced, will bring those who act on them closer to fulfilling their God-given destinies.

Extra copies of this book and *What's in a Name* are available at www.amazon.com.

Your local bookstore may order them from www.wordalive.ca.

For further information or to contact Fay, please visit www.fayrowe.com.

Praise for *What's in a Name*

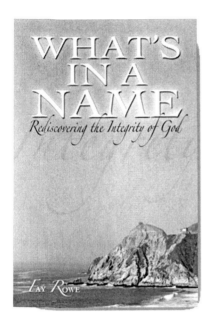

"This book is brilliantly simple, surprisingly deep, and clearly understandable. *What's in a Name* reveals an intelligent gospel for an intelligent world!"

~Lorne Rostotski
Past Director,
Faith Christian Fellowship,
Canada

"I feel privileged and very blessed to have had your manuscript put into my hands. It is a profound, well documented piece, equal in both its scholarly and spiritual merits."

~Dr Norrel London
Professor Emeritus, University of Western Ontario

"The connection with the reader is very effective. The reader is drawn in completely. You have a wonderful piece of insight to share."

~Reviewer
The Writer's Edge Manuscript Service

"A wonderful read; it challenged me. Even though I'm 80 it put excitement in my heart! Thank you so much for writing this book."

~Beth Burdick
Reader

Printed in the United States
111890LV00002B/46-66/P

9 781897 373149